A Trial Lawyer's Case Directory
November 1958 – 1995

By
Tom Coghill

NO PART OF THIS BOOK may be reproduced in any form or by any means (electronically or mechanically, including photocopy, recording or any information retrieval system) without written permission of the author. The author has full ownership and legal right to publish all the materials in this book.

All rights reserved.

Lawyer and author John Grisham wrote in his book *The Street Lawyer*:

> *"No one joined a large firm with a goal of becoming a real estate lawyer. There were far more glamorous arenas in which to establish reputations. Litigation was the all-time favorite, and the litigators were still the most revered of all God's lawyers…"*

When I enrolled at the University of Missouri – Columbia in 1944, I intended to follow a course that would be best suited for politics – Political Science, History, and Law, which I knew would be disrupted by military service during World War II. Following voluntary service as an enlisted man in the U.S. Navy, I returned to Mizzou and secured a law degree in February 1950, and returned to my hometown, Farmington, Missouri where I opened a one room solo law office intent on being elected the next Prosecuting Attorney. During that year by court appointment and with no fee, I defended a murder case and bank robbery case – lost both of them and lost the election.

At age 23, following a waiver of the 25 age requirement, I became a Special Agent in J. Edgar Hoover's FBI fighting Communism and Brinks robbers in Boston. Thereafter, I practiced primarily as a civil defense trial lawyer with firms in eastern Missouri, trying cases from St. Louis to Cape Girardeau and handling appeals and arguing in the Missouri Supreme Court and St. Louis Court of Appeals. I tried many cases during this time but kept no particular record of the cases.

On September 1, 1958, I became a member of the firm of Pope and Driemeyer in East St. Louis, Illinois, which ultimately became part of Thompson Coburn, a multi-state law firm. This was the industrial area of St. Louis and very litigious. East St. Louis was located in St. Clair County and the primary litigation took place in St. Clair County and adjoining Madison County.

St. Clair County was dubbed by the media as "Plaintiffs Paradise" and Madison County was dubbed as Judicial Hell Hole #1, while St. Clair County was dubbed Judicial Hell Hole #2.

So how does one become one of "the most revered of all God's lawyers…" as described by John Grisham?

Clarence Darrow was my hero lawyer and idol. To me being a real lawyer was a lawyer who tried cases in court before a jury. But, how does one get the cases – through reputation! Lawyers could not advertise in my day. You started with nothing and gradually built a reputation. Trying lawsuits is combat law and you are eventually judged as one would judge a professional baseball pitcher. A 20 game season winner is in high demand and a 3 game winner is looking for a job in the minors.

I was blessed, and yes, lucky in my trial career starting November 1, 1958 and ending on December 31, 1995, on what was referred to as the East Side (Illinois). I successfully defended U-Haul in a multimillion dollar lawsuit in a three and one-half month trial which set a record for trial length in Southern Illinois at the time and I received a verdict of $350,000.00 for a young man injured in a motorcycle accident which was a record high verdict in St. Clair County at the time.

Ultimately my clients included, among others, General Motors Corporation, International Harvester, Nissan, Volkswagen, Toyota, U-Haul, Mitsubishi, Audi, Americo, Joy Technologies, Diamond-Star Motor, Peabody Coal Company, Montgomery Elevator Company, AH Robbins, Upjohn, Sterling Drug, SC Johnson & Son, Pfizer, Inc., Up-Right, Inc., Kimberly Clark, Honda, Monterey Coal Company, Exxon, Singer Company, Winthrop Laboratories, The Bayer Company, National Mine Service, Lee Norse Company, Ingersoll-Rand, Snyder General Corporation, Breon Laboratories, Winthrop Stearns Laboratories, Continental Can Company, Outboard Marine Corporation, Freightliner Corporation, AB Chance Company, Granite City Steel, Zeigler Coal Company, Clark Oil & Refining Company, General Electric Company, Dunlop Tire & Rubber Corporation, Canada Dry Corporation, Long-Airdox Company, Hyster Company, Monroe Shock Absorber, Marquip, Inc., Cushman Motors, Terex , Shell Oil Company, New York Central Railroad, Alton and Southern Railroad,

Nickel Plate Railroad, Norfolk and Western Railroad, Penn Central Railroad, Illinois Central Railroad, The Baltimore and Ohio Railroad Co., GM&O Railroad, Missouri Pacific Railroad, Wabash Railroad, Terminal Railroad Association, Obear Nester Glass Co., Swift Packing Co., Hunter Packing Co., Laclede Steel Co., Kerr-Magee Corp., Winthrop Laboratories, Inc., Stihl, Inc., Union Electric Co., Massey-Ferguson, Inc., Otis Elevator Co., Kentucky Fried Chicken, Emerson electric Co., Helene Curtis Industries, Inc., American Zinc Co., National Steel Corp., Toyota Industrial Trucks, U.S.A., Chrysler Corp., Gates Rubber Co., Cushman Motors, Ishab Corporation, Mobay Corporation, Toyotomi Kogyo Co, Ltd., Toyotomi America, Inc., White Farm Equipment Co., Louisiana Towing Co., Inc., May Stores Shopping Centers., Inc., Sioux City and New Orleans Barge Lines, Inc., Hyster Company, John Deere Company, Eagle Marine Industries, Inc. and National Lead Co.

Client Locations

It did not take long for me to realize that I could not keep track of these cases or handle them alone, so I devised an index card system to keep track of the cases. Each card included the caption of the case, the amount of the suit, the adverse attorney, a file number, a cause number, trial date, and factual summary. In addition, I picked a team for each case. I was lead trial lawyer on most of the cases and usually designated a research lawyer, motions lawyer, pleading lawyer, discovery lawyer and associate trial lawyer.

Upon receipt of each new case, we commenced the Discovery: Interrogatories (questions to be answered under oath), Requests to Produce (requirement of production under oath of all material documents, etc.), Motion to Admit Relevant Facts (nothing related to the product failed, you were intoxicated, etc.), prepared pleadings attacking plaintiff's complaint or petition if appropriate and depositions of all parties and identified witnesses which usually required trips throughout the U.S.

Once a deposition was taken, we would forward a letter summary to the client at the earliest possible time. When all discovery had been completed, I would forward an evaluation letter to the client reviewing all of the anticipated testimony and other evidence, estimating our chance of success or failure with an estimate of verdict range and recommendations for trial or settlement. And then – War! The trial begins!

The remainder of this booklet consists of the index cards of the cases referred to me by clients from November, 1958 to December 31, 1995. The book was prepared and assembled simply for posterity's sake with the thought that some descendant or another "…most revered of all God's Lawyers…" will find this directory of case cards to be of interest.

By actual count I received 1,248 cases during this time period. Only 416 of the cases are included in this booklet.

During my overall career as a trial lawyer, I received cases pending in the following locations:

In Missouri

City	Population
St. Louis	396,700
Clayton	13,900
Steelville	1,500
St. Charles	54,600
St. Joseph	71,900
Hillsboro	1,600
Liberty	20,500
Oregon	900
Farmington	11,600
Fredericktown	4,000
Jackson	9,300
Cape Girardeau	34,400
Ste. Genevieve	4,400
Potosi	2,700
Ironton	1,500
New Madrid	3,400
Marble Hill	1,400
Poplar Bluff	17,000
Jefferson City	35,500
Perryville	6,900

Missouri Lawsuit Locations

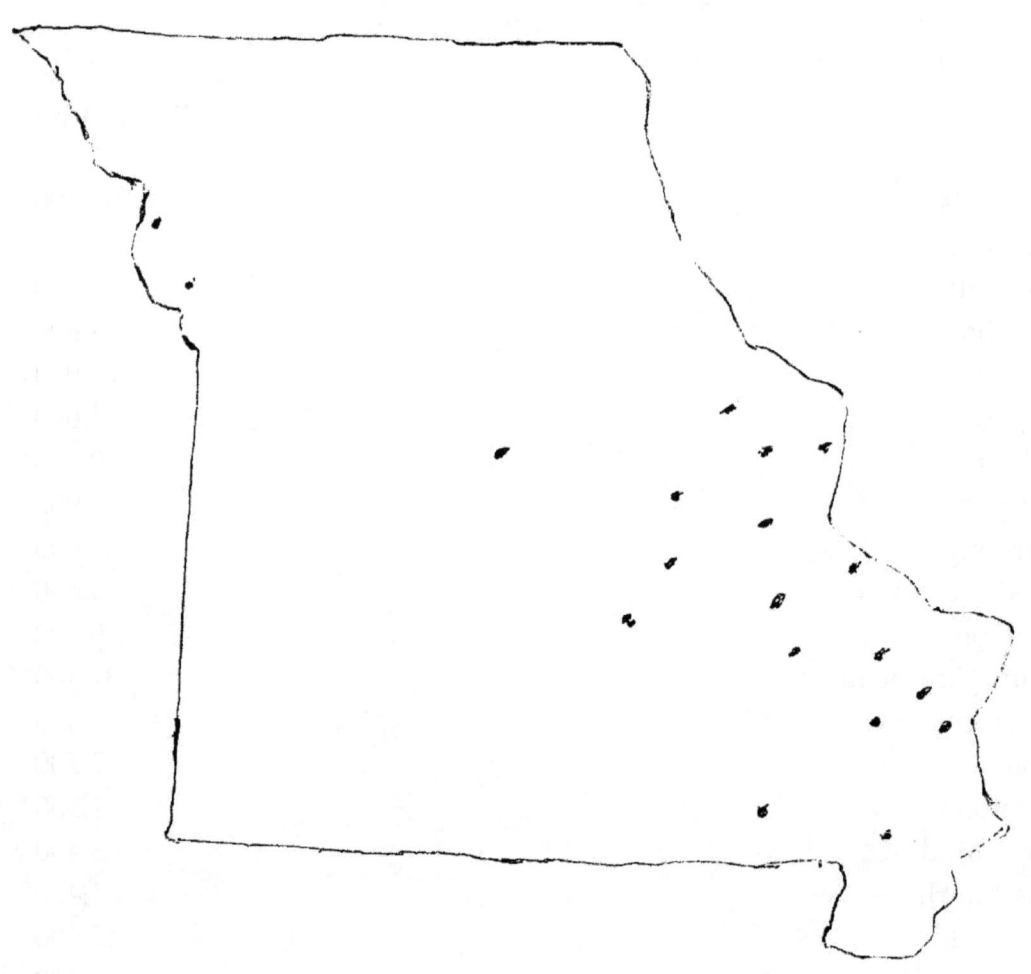

In Illinois

County	City	Population
Bond	Greenville	4,800
Macoupin	Carlinville	5,400
Sangamon	Springfield	105,400
Jefferson	Mt. Vernon	17,000
Randolph	Chester	8,200
Franklin	Benton	17,200
	Shelbyville	4,900
Scott	Winchester	1,800
	Charleston	20,400
	East St. Louis	40,900
Williamson	Marion	14,500
Montgomery	Hillsboro	4,400
Vermillion	Danville	33,800
	Edwardsville	14,600
Monroe	Waterloo	5,100
McLean	Bloomington	51,900
Perry	Pinckneyville	3,400
Jersey	Jerseyville	7,400
Marion	Salem	7,500
Clinton	Carlyle	3,500
Jackson	Murphysboro	9,200
Union	Jonesboro	1,700
Henry	Cambridge	2,100
Cook	Chicago	2,783,700
Effingham	Effingham	11,900
Wayne	Fairfield	5,400
Wabash	Mt. Carmel	8,300
White	Carmi	5,600

County	City	Population
Coles	Mattoon	18,400
	Alton	32,900
	Granite City	32,800
	Madison	4,600
	Belleville	42,800
	Edwardsville	14,600

Illinois Lawsuit Locations

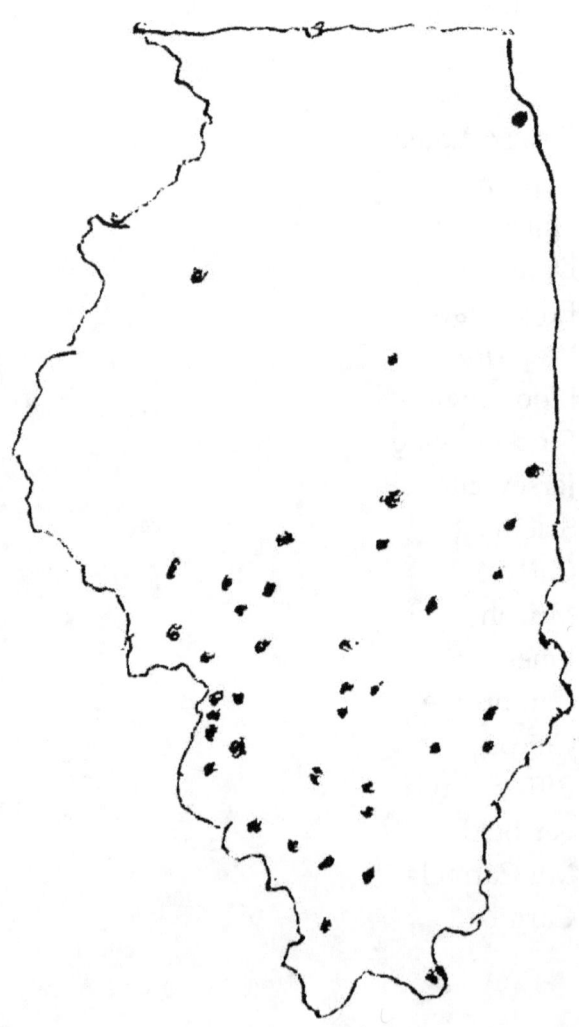

The following is what my law firm prepared about me to entice clients:

W. THOMAS COGHILL, JR.
Chairman – Product Liability Litigation Section
Thompson & Mitchell

Tom Coghill is nationally recognized as a skillful product liability court room defense lawyer. His legal career started almost 40 years ago. He accelerated his academic studies by completing a four year high school curriculum in three years and a six year law degree curriculum in four and one-half years. His college education was interrupted with service in the United States Navy as an enlisted man, having volunteered at the age of 17. He received his LL.B degree (subsequently replaced with a J.D. degree) from the University of Missouri-Columbia in 1950. Although he was only 22 years of age when he received his law degree, being the youngest member of his class, he was chosen by the members of the Phi Alpha Delta Law Fraternity to be its Justice (President).

Following graduation from law school, Coghill returned to his home town in Missouri where he opened his own office for the general practice of law. In 1951 he left this practice to become a Special Agent with the Federal Bureau of Investigation. While with the FBI he was assigned to the Washington, D.C., Boston, and Detroit offices.

Upon leaving the FBI, Coghill returned to a small law firm in his home town in Missouri where he engaged in the general practice of law. He was primarily responsible for litigation matters and tried jury cases of all types and handled appeals in the appellate level courts.

In 1957 Coghill became an associate with a St. Louis law firm in order to devote full time to trial practice. The litigation he handled was primarily defense oriented and included representation of railroads and insurance companies.

Since 1958 Coghill has practiced as a defense lawyer representing large corporations in the plaintiff oriented high verdict area of Illinois just across the Mississippi River from St. Louis. He has defended numerous railroads under various Federal Statutes as well as Admiralty cases. He has also defended major corporations who have been sued for violation of the Illinois Structural Work Act. His experience also includes defending physicians and health care providers against malpractice claims. His firm, Pope and Driemeyer, merged with Thompson & Mitchell on January 1, 1985.

The first case he defended in Illinois was against Alan Dixon, presently a United States Senator from the State of Illinois. Coghill's intoxicated client rear-ended the plaintiff's automobile when she was attempting to make a left turn into her driveway. The jury verdict was for the defendant.

The case of <u>Sloter v. New York Central Railroad Company</u> was unique in that not only did Coghill secure a defendant's verdict for the railroad but he recovered the full measure of damages for the train which had been wrecked by plaintiff's decedent in a grade crossing accident in the State of Ohio. The suit was brought by James Dooley of Chicago who was seeking millions of dollars under a treble damage statute in Ohio. Dooley later became a Justice of the Supreme Court of the State of Illinois,

For the last 23 years, since Illinois adopted strict liability in tort in 1965 in the case of <u>Suvada v. White Motor Company</u>, Coghill has devoted practically all of his time defending manufacturers in product liability cases. These manufacturers have included General Motors Corporation, International Harvester Company (Navistar), Volkswagen (U.S.A. and German), Nissan (U.S.A. and Japan), Toyota (U.S.A. and Japan), Tokio Marine (a product liability insurer), U-Haul, Joy Technologies Inc., Lucas-Girling of the United Kingdom, Long-Airdox Company, Upjohn, Sterling Drug Company, Elkins-Sirm, Inc., A. H. Robbins, S. C. Johnson Company, Kimberly-Clark, Outboard Marine Corporation, Toyotomi Kogyo and Toyotomi American, Freightliner Corporation, National Mine Service, Montgomery Elevator Company, General Electric Company, and others. Some of the noteworthy cases are discussed below.

After U-Haul was found liable for a then national record-setting award of $5 million punitive damages, Coghill was selected to defend it in similar cases brought by the same plaintiff attorney. In a three and one-half month trial, which set a record for trial length in Southern Illinois at the time, the court granted U-Haul a directed verdict at the conclusion of plaintiff's case. Plaintiff's original $20 million demand was thereafter disposed of for $100,000.00 to avoid further litigation expense. Michael Shoen, an attorney and son of the founder of U-Haul, worked with Coghill in connection with this case. John Haberstad of the State of Washington was one of U-Haul's many experts. Gerald Driefke of St. Louis was plaintiff's expert.

Coghill's success for GM is unblemished in the high verdict area where he handles their cases. One such case was the case of Prediger v. GM in which a 16 year old attractive paraplegic female sued General Motors Corporation alleging a defective disc brake design which was used on millions of GM vehicles. Plaintiff's expert, Paul O'Shea, formerly of Newport Beach, California and presently from San Diego, testified that the design was defective because it lacked shielding to prevent rocks or gravel from wedging into the mechanism, O'Shea presented movies of testing done by him demonstrating this phenomenon. The trial resulted in a defendant's verdict. GM's in-house lawyer was David Collins and GM's in-house engineer was Carl Granthen and its outside experts were Donald Huelke of Ann Arbor, Michigan and J. Stannard Baker of the Traffic Institute of Northwestern University,

A wrongful death case was successfully defended involving the steering system of an Oldsmobile in the case of Samotis v. GM. The decedent's husband, a Colonel with the United States Air Force, claimed that his new Oldsmobile with 900 miles on the odometer veered off of the highway resulting in a collision with a concrete pylon and the death of his wife. David Flescher was the in-house GM engineer and John Piccin was the in-house GM lawyer. James Booth, formerly with the Buick Division of GM, and Joe Harris, formerly with GM, were two of the plaintiff's many experts.

The case of Smith v. GM involved the energy absorbing steering column of a Cadillac. This is the same column used in millions of GM vehicles. Plaintiff's counsel claimed it was defectively designed and, as a result, plaintiff claimed that her husband sustained a ruptured aorta when his chest impacted the steering wheel and steering column resulting in his death. Carl Savage, David Foust, and Bill Chichowski were GM's in-house experts and Don Parshall was the in-house lawyer. The jury verdict was for GM.

In <u>Marotta v. GM</u> the jury returned a verdict for GM where the plaintiff truck driver claimed that the battery box step design of a GM truck was defective causing him to fall and sustain serious injuries. Plaintiff's expert was Dr. Gerald Driefke of St. Louis and GM's in-house experts were Carl F. Jansen and Carl Savage. GM's in-house lawyer was Don Parshall. Although the jury returned a verdict in favor of GM, the trial judge refused to enter judgment on the verdict until he was ordered to do so by the Supreme Court of the State of Illinois.

<u>Engelman v. GM</u> involved a Pontiac which had been subject to recall to add a shield to protect the steering mechanism. The recall letter indicated that it might be impossible to steer the vehicle should rocks become lodged in the mechanism. The vehicle left the roadway, collided with a tree, and the driver and passenger were severely injured. The recall letter was received at the driver's house two days following the accident. The recall letter and recall Information were admitted into evidence by the trial court. The verdict was in favor of GM. Jerry A. Confer was the in-house engineer for GM and David Collins was the in-house lawyer for GM.

Three cases have been successfully defended for GM where it was claimed that an axle failed resulting in a separation of a wheel from the automobile. The case of <u>Markovitch v.GM</u> involved a rear-end collision when plaintiff's automobile was struck by a Pontiac. Because of the severity of the accident it was investigated by many police officers and firemen, all of whom were called by and testified in behalf of plaintiff. Most of the police officers were permitted to reconstruct the accident and they opined that a wheel had separated from the Pontiac causing the accident. Plaintiff's expert was Ben Eiayse, a Professor at the University of Missouri-St. Louis, and a metallurgist employed by McDonnell-Douglas Aircraft: Company. Plaintiff claimed metal fatigue. GM's in-house experts were Edward Reynolds and Ken Orlowski, GM also called upon Thomas Dolan of the University of Illinois-Champaign. The verdict was for GM.

In Suydam v. GM the product was a Vega automobile which had been subject to a recall because of C-lock problems which could result in the separation of an axle and a wheel. The accident involved, a head-on collision between plaintiff's automobile and the Vega. Two independent eye witnesses following the Vega testified they saw the left rear wheel separate from the Vega after which the Vega veered to the left, crossed the centerline, and collided with plaintiff's approaching automobile head-on. Plaintiff's expert was H. Boulter Kelsey, Jr., a mechanical engineer from Sb. Louis, as well as a metallurgical engineer and other experts. Plaintiff claimed metal fatigue. GM's in-house expert was Ray J. Schultz. The jury returned a verdict in favor of GM.

In a case tried last October, McCain v. GM, plaintiff claimed she sustained injuries resulting in $500,000 in medical bills when her new Oldsmobile left the highway. The right rear wheel was separated from the automobile and some distance beyond where the Oldsmobile came to rest. Plaintiff's expert, H. Boulter Kelsey, Jr., criticized the design of the manner in which the axle tubes are attached to the vehicle and the fact that there are no outboard retention devices in the event of an axle failure. Edward Reynolds was the in-house engineer who testified in behalf of GM. The verdict was for GM.

Other GM engineers with whom Coghill has worked or consulted include Dick Maiers, Bob Nagel, Kirk Ulman, Walter Zych, Jerry Chiddister, Bill Chichowski, Ron Elwell, Mike Holcomb, Jim Holden, Al McKeen (who now operates an independent consulting firm), Ray Reske, Carl Savage, Bob Smith, Art Vansteelandt, Doug VanSweeden, E'ick Stewart and others. Members of GM Legal Staff with whom Coghill has worked include, Charles W. Babcock, B. Lynn Enderby, Patricia Harris, Donald R. Parshall, Jr., Jay Hollis, Don Schiemann, Douglas Toering, Howard Silverman, and others no longer with the product liability department.

The Nissan cases have involved primarily crashworthiness claims. One post-collision fuel-fed fire case was settled on the eve of trial very satisfactorily to Nissan. Plaintiff's primary experts were Paul O'Shea from California and Frederick Arndt from Tempe, Arizona. Nissan's independent experts were Bob Cromack from Tempe, Arizona and John Haberstad from the State of Washington. (<u>Hastings v. Nissan</u>). In <u>Medley v. Nissan</u> the door latch design and crashworthiness of a Datsun 3210 was the issue. The plaintiff was a brain damaged quadriplegic. Plaintiff's experts were Frederick Arndt of Tempe, Arizona and Robert Brenner, former director of NHTSA, of Rockville, Maryland together with Bruce Enz. Defendant's experts were Dick Stewart, former GM engineer from Michigan, Bob Cromack of Tempe, Arizona, and Don Huelke of the University of Michigan. Bob Yakushi was the in-house engineer for Nissan. Steve Lending was the in-house lawyer for Nissan. The case was very satisfactorily settled on behalf of Nissan on the first day of trial. Other experts with whom Coghill has dealt in handling Nissan cases include Pete Jasich of Costa Mesa, California, Lee Carr of Houston, Failure Analysis Associates of Phoenix and others.

Volkswagen cases have all been crashworthiness cases. These cases have included the Type II Van and the Type I Beetle. The issue of oversteer and understeer has also been involved. Frederick Arndt of Tempe, Arizona and Paul O'Shea of California, The Institute for Automotive Safety of Rockville, Maryland and John Noettl of Scottsdale, Arizona have been involved on the plaintiff's side. Experts involved on the defendant's side have included G. Murray Mackay of Birmingham, England, Charles Warner, Ronald Woolley and Tom Perl of Orem, Utah, and in-house engineers from both the U.S.A. arid German companies. The last Volkswagen case tried was in November of 1988 involving a young male paraplegic. Immediately before closing arguments, following a six week trial, plaintiff settled with co-defendants and confessed VW's motion for mistrial. Subsequently, plaintiff's counsel agreed to dismiss the case against Volkswagen without payment.

More than 40 cases are presently being defended for Joy Technologies Inc. involving their shuttle cars. (Joy is the world's largest manufacturer of underground mining equipment.) Plaintiff's theory of liability is to the effect that the design of Joy's shuttle car is inherently unreasonably dangerous resulting in an unusually rough ride causing ruptured discs and other spinal injuries. Plaintiff's experts are H. Boulter

Kelsey, Jr. of St. Louis and John Dahle of San Francisco. Defendant's experts are Edward Caulfield of Packer Engineering in Naperville, Illinois, Dr. Harry Smith who is with Dr. James Benedict of San Antonio, Texas, Dr. Will Fairley (a statistician) of Philadelphia, Leon Kazarian of Dayton, Ohio, and others. Plaintiff's flagship case was tried in the United States District Court in Alton in January and February of this year and resulted in a defendant's verdict.

An insecticide case involving Raid Flea Killer manufactured by S. C. Johnson & Son, Inc. of Racine, Wisconsin is scheduled to go to trial in September. The 11 year old plaintiff claims that he sustained total paralysis, except for his eyelids, as a result of exposure to the product. Plaintiff's experts include Dr. Neil Allen of Highland Park, Illinois, Dr. Mark Thoman of Des Moines, Iowa, Dr. Wallace D. Winters of the University of California-Davis Dr. Wendell Kilgore of the University of California-Davis, Dr. Christopher Long, Toxicologist, of Chesterfield, Missouri, Dr. Robert Cunitz, an ergonomist and human factors expert, and others. Defendant's experts include Dr. Herbert Schaumburg of Albert Einstein College of Medicine in New York, Dr. Maurice Victor, Distinguished Physician with Veterans Administration Hospital in White River Junction, Vermont, Dr. John Doull of the University of Kansas Medical School, and Charles Porterfield, Bioengineer from San Antonio, Texas.

Cases which Coghill has tried to conclusion have involved the technical fields of mechanical engineering, chemical engineering, petroleum engineering, ergonomics, bioengineering, pharmaceutical products arid devices, flammable fabrics, industrial engineering, aeronautical engineering, structural engineering, design engineering, metallurgical engineering, failure analysis, automobile design, farm equipment design, mining equipment design, and trailer design, together with all of the specialty fields in the medical profession including toxicology, pharmacology, and epidemiology. Coghill has also participated in the orchestration of crash testing including frontal and rear-end barrier tests, sled tests, and roll-over tests. He has been involved in computerized accident reconstruction and photogrammetry. He has been involved in various fire testing for vehicles and flammable fabrics testing. He has been involved in various dynamic stability tests and mathematical modeling.

By invitation, Coghill attended Specialized Product Liability Seminars sponsored by Volkswagen in New York and in Florida and one sponsored by Toyota in California. He has worked with Eric Taira, an in-house lawyer with Toyota.

Coghill is a Fellow of the American College of Trial Lawyers, and Member of The American Bar Association, Missouri State Bar Association, Illinois State Bar Association, Bar Association of Metropolitan St. Louis, St. Clair County Bar Association, East St. Louis Bar Association, National Association of Railroad Trial Counsel, Illinois Association of Defense Trial Counsel, Defense Research Institute, and a charter member of the Fellows of the Illinois Bar Association. He is listed in Who's Who of the Midwest, Who's Who in American Law, Who's Who in the World, Who's What and Why in Missouri, and Dictionary of International Biography, 1971, Seventh Edition published in England. He received an AV Preeminent Award from the Peer Review Rating process of Martindale-Hubbell which is the highest rating in both legal ability and ethical standards. By appointment of the Supreme Court of Illinois he has served as Chairman of a three Member hearing board for the Illinois Registration and Disciplinary Commission for many years. He is co-author of *Illinois Products Liability* and author of *Cavaliers*, a historical novel.

Case Directory

HOOVER, HARVEY v ALEXANDER, HUGH R.
(Security)
Amount of Suit: $25,000.00
Attorney: Edward Moorman
File No.:   8-25-49876 Steitz
Cause No.:   65-2199 Circuit Court St. Clair County
Set for Trial: 4/17/1967
Summary: Date of Accident: 10/10/1964. 84 year old Plaintiff trespassing on Defendant's property attempted to cross footbridge and fell. Plaintiff's attorney demanded $48,57.12. Defendant offered $750.

JOHNSON, LARRY v GRANITE CITY STEEL COMPANY
(Safeco)
Amount of Suit: $10,000.00
Attorney: Beatty, Schooley and Theis
File No.:   BLP 259733 Noble
Cause No.:   65-L-763 Circuit Court Madison County
Summary: Date of Accident: 9/1/1965. Scaffold Act case. Granite City Steel Co. Plaintiff fell from roof of a building under construction.

REEVES, CLEO v MOTOR TRANSPORTATION COMPANY, et al
(Hartford)
Amount of Suit: $10,000.00
Attorney: Wagner, Conner, et al
File No.:   46 Kal 20258 Yoakam
Cause No.:   69-2007 Circuit Court St. Clair County
Summary: Date of Accident: 10/31/1967. 3:30 PM I-270, Madison County, IL. Plaintiff, operating tractor trailer unit west on I-70 rear ended by Defendant's tractor trailer unit. Defendant arrested.

EDWARDS, RUSSELL L. v CARGILL v HANKS, STANLEY
(Hartford)
Amount of Suit: $50,000.00
Attorney: P - Chapman, Strawn; 3P - Howard Boman
File No.:   HO1050L1565 Cutkomp
Cause No.:   65-L-500 CircuitCourt Madison County
Set for Trial: 2/27/1965
Summary: Date of Accident: 6/15/1965. 10:00 AM at Cargill Mills in Granite City. Defendant had contract to paint, etc. at Carghill. Plaintiff, an employee of Hanks, injured while performing contract. Third Plaintiff sues for express indemnity.

HARRELL, BILL v S.M. WILSON & CO., et al
(Maryland Casual Co.)
Amount of Suit: $100,000.00
Attorney: Hillary Hallett
File No.:   560-L-16391 Swanston
Cause No.:   65-L-602 CircuitCourt Madison County
Set for Trial: 12/11/1965
Summary: Date of Accident: Jan/Feb 1965. Scaffold Act case. Plaintiff, an employee of Pope Corp, working on erection of freezer box in Alton, IL, struck on head by scaffolding boards.

LLOYD, JOANN, et al v CELUCOAT CORPORATION, et al
(Commercial Union)
Amount of Suit: Count I - $75,000; Count II - $25,000;
Count III - $25,000, Count IV - $25,000;
Count V - $25,000; Count Vi - $25,000;
Count VII - $75,000
Attorney: Cohn, Cohn and Korein
File No.: 29-140412 John Steffens, Chicago
Cause No.: 68-8244 St. Clair County
Summary: Date of Accident: 8/12/1967. 5:45 AM Interstate Highway, Will County, IL, southwest of Joliet. 11 vehicles involved. All vehicles traveling north when lead vehicles stopped because of dense fog and others piled up to rear. Defendant shipped inflammablbe paint on one truck which was struck in rear causing flames to spread over area.

SHEPHEARD, WARREN D. v LOVELACE TRUCK SERVICE
(Royal-Globe)
Amount of Suit: $75,000.00
Attorney: John Hoban
File No.: Q654A-08839 English
Cause No.: 65-124 US District Court, E. St. Louis
Set for Trial: 2/14/1966
Summary: Date of Accident: 7/1/1964. Certain-Teed Products Co., 1700 E. Broadway, E. St. Louis, IL. Defendant's truck started to leave with load of shingles at 3:30 PM and shingles fell off. Plaintiff, an employee of Certain-Teed, attempting to help in some manner, caught left hand resulting in hand being crushed.

LAUTNER, KEITH, a minor, etc. v KEELEY BROS. CONTRACTING COMPANY, et al (American Mutual)
Amount of Suit: $25,000.00
Attorney: William Schooley
File No.: CGL 052446-00-257-241591 Stewart
Cause No.: 68-L-509 CircuitCourt Madison County
Summary: Date of Accident: 7/2/1962. Dorcas Drive, Cahokia, IL. Plaintiff, riding his bicycle, claimes he struck a hole on Dorcas Drive. Plaintiff claims that the hole resulted from work having been done by Defendant.

COCHRAN, WILLIAM D. v S.M. WILSON & CO., et al (Maryland Casualty)
Amount of Suit: $150,000.00
Attorney: Johnson, Ducey & Feder
File No.: 560-L-18943 Matheny
Cause No.: 68-L-360 Circuit Court Madison County
Summary: Date of Accident: 5/18/1967. Scaffold Act case at Nestle Co., Granite City, IL.

BECKER, LULU, et al v AA SAV CORP. (Hartford)
Amount of Suit: Count I - $50,000; Count II - $25,000
Attorney: C.C. Dreman
File No.: 46 I 40949 Yoakam
Cause No.: 69-2297 Circuit Court St. Clair County
Summary: Date of Accident: 10/15/1968. Sav Mart, Carlyle Road, Belleville, IL. Plaintiff, a customer, slipped and fell on popcorn.

WALL, JUANITA M., Admr. V SIU, et al
(Security)
Amount of Suit: $100,000.00
Attorney: Green and Hoagland
File No.:   1-01-20123 Ray Evers
Cause No.:   66-L-848
Summary: Date of Accident: 5/11/1965. Wrongful death action. 12:50 PM, SIU Campus. Deceased, employee of Bituminous, electrocuted when crane cable came in contact with high voltage wire. SIU being sued for failure to furnish a safe place to work.

YATES, LESLIE v LEONE, RUDOLPH, et al
(Security)
Amount of Suit: $100,000.00
Attorney: Paul L. Pratt
File No.:   1-01-24298 Atkins
Cause No.:   67-L-189 CircuitCourt Madison County
Summary: Date of Accident: 8/23/1966. First Baptist Church - Gillespie, IL. Defendants, delivering ready-mixed cement to construction site. Plaintiff, a carpenter, claims some splashed into his eyes.

PELO, WILLARD v WILBUR WAGGONER EQUIPMENT
(Hartford)
Amount of Suit: $100,000.00
Attorney: William Schooley
File No.:   Yoakam
Cause No.:   69-L-555 CircuitCourt Madison County
Summary: Date of Accident: 9/20/1968. Granite City Steel Co., Granite City, IL. Plaintiff, an ironworker employed by Nooter Corporation. Defendant contracted to furnish truck and driver to Granite City Steel Co. Plaintiff fell off truck when it started suddenly.

DOSSIE, KING v N&W RAILWAY CO.
Amount of Suit: $75,000.00
Attorney: Chapman, Strawn, Kinder & Talbert
File No.: 161-3863 Sample
Cause No.: 68-9835 Circuit Court St. Clair County
Summary: Date of Accident: 4/6/1968. Brooklyn Yards. Plaintiff, a laborer, claims he strained back.

DOERGE v WABASH RAILROAD
Amount of Suit: $560,000.00
Attorney: Bock & Stenger
File No.: 161-3420 Sample
Cause No.: 65-2145 Circuit Court St. Clair County
Summary: Date of Accident: 4/21/1963. FELA Case - Brooklyn Yard. Plaintiff, an engineer on train which collided with Terminal train which was on wrong track. On 6/22/63 Plaintiff, walking across train table stepped on rotten board.

BROWN, ROSE v MISSOURI PACIFIC TRUCK COMPANY, et al (Hartford)
Amount of Suit: $15,000.00
Attorney: Listeman, Bandy & Hamilton
File No.: 46AL37993 Greer
Cause No.: 68-9233 Circuit Court St. Clair County
Summary: Date of Accident: 7/1/1968. 4:30 PM at Korner Grill, 3295 Mississippi Avenue, Cahokia, IL. Defendant's trailer being pulled by tractor owned by Newman Drayage and operated by Co-Defendant Washburn, struck Korner Grill in which Plaintiff was seated.

McGEE, RENATA PATRICE v DILLARD, JAMES
(Manchester Insurance & Indemnity Co.)
Amount of Suit: $50,000.00
Attorney: Melvin Trotier
File No.:   A5 01 13 Blackwell
Cause No.:   69-1654 Circuit Court St. Clair County
Summary: Date of Accident: 3/13/1969. 4:15 PM at an alley in John DeShields Homes Housing Development, E. St. Louis. 6 year old Plaintiff was a pedestrian crossing the alley when she was struck by Defendant's southbound automobile.

TURNER, WILLIE v NORFOLK & WESTERN RAILWAY CO.
Amount of Suit: $150,000.00
Attorney: Chapman, Talbert & Chapman
File No.:   71-L-245 CircuitCourt Madison County
Set for Trial: 8/15/1969
Summary: Date of Accident: Brooklyn Yards. Plaintiff, a carman, injured his back while carrying a knuckle.

GRAY, RAYMOND v. SCHWEICKERT, ELLIOTT, et al Millitzer Security
Amount of Suit: $60,000.00
Attorney: Russell Classen
File No.:   8-25-50897 Atkins
Cause No.:   67-5421 Circuit Court St. Clair County
Summary: Date of Accident: 1/16/1965. 4:30 PM in front of assds premises at 11 W C Street, Belle. Plaintiff, walking on sidewalk, slipped and fell on ice caused by drain from Defendant's property. Plaintiff demanded $30,000, Defendant offered $5,000.

HORN, HOMER LEE v BARCLAY TERMINAL WAREHOUSE, et al (Employers Commercial Union)
Amount of Suit: $200,000.00
Attorney: Edward Neville
File No.: K4-680-1 McWilliams
Cause No.: 69-159 Circuit Court St. Clair County
Summary: Date of Accident: 6/25/1969. Plaintiff, an employee of Nestle Co. in Granite City, IL, opened a door to a boxcar and was injured when a T chest fell from the boxcar. Plaintiff sues Co-Defendant, IL Central RR, and insured charging that insured negligently loaded the boxcar.

McCASLAND, WILLIAM v MONSANTO v CORRIGAN CO.
(Hartford) (See also McCasland, Wm. V Corrigan)
Amount of Suit: $10,000.00
Attorney: P - Robert Godfrey; Monstanto- Brady, Donovan
File No.: 66-5059 Circuit Court Belleville
Summary: Date of Accident: Third Party Complaint.

BREWER, JIMMIE v NORFOLK & WESTERN RAILWAY CO.
Amount of Suit: $100,000.00
Attorney: Morris B. Chapman
File No.: 161-3763 Sample
Cause No.: 68-8362 Circuit Court St. Clair County
Summary: Date of Accident: 2/15/1968. FELA case at Madison Yards of Defendant. Plaintiff, a carman, tripped over air line cut-off valve alongside #4 track as he was attempting to couple air hoses.

BAY, JUNE, Admr. V GENERAL ELECTRIC, et al
(Employers Commercial Union)
Amount of Suit: $225,000.00
Attorney: Coleman, Ross & Cekovsky
File No.:   K4-966 McWilliams
Cause No.:   Circuit Court City of St. Louis
Summary: Date of Accident: 11/10/1969. Wrongful death action. 8:50 PM, IL Highway 146 four miles east of Anna, IL. Deceased, a passenger in an automobile operated by Defendant which left the highway and hit a tree.

MOD-CO, INC. v PUR-GAS, INC., et al
(Commercial Union) (See Patrick v Pur-Gas)
Amount of Suit: $13,000.00
Attorney: Chapman, Strawn & Kinder
File No.:   46-12299-1 McWilliams
Cause No.:   66-L-465 CircuitCourt Madison County
Summary: Date of Accident: 10/8/1965. 5:30 AM Rural Route, Edwards. Property damage suit. As tenant started to light furnace the home exploded destroying residence. Defendant is LP gas supplier.

ELLEDGE, RUBY v WALLACE, RICHARD, et al
(Continental Insurance Company)
Amount of Suit: $24,625.75
Attorney: John E. Norton
File No.:   Daly
Cause No.:   69-905 Circuit Court St. Clair County
Summary: Date of Accident: 8/23/1967. Castle Haven Convalescent Center, 225 Castellano Drive, Swansea, IL. Plaintiff claims she fell on Defendant's property.

HOWELLS, EDWIN, Adm. etc. v H&M SPORTING GOODS (Lumbermens Mutual)
Amount of Suit: $100,000.00
Attorney: Massa and Williams
File No.: Ruedlinger
Cause No.: 68-I-419 CircuitCourt Madison County
Summary: Death action. 17 year old deceased purchased .22 caliber revolver from Defendant and later accidently shot himself.

GEASCHEL, ADOLPH E. v MILLER, LARRY, et al (Hartford)
Amount of Suit: $20,000.00
Attorney: Brady, Donovan & Hatch
File No.: HO 150 LP 53149 Lane
Cause No.: 69-26 Circuit Court St. Clair County
Summary: Date of Accident: 1/27/1968. Central and Southern property in Caseyville, IL. Defendant's got onto tractor and started it and ran into Plaintiff's property.

FERRELL, BETTY v MYRA JEAN TALKINGTON (Safeco)
Amount of Suit: $10,000.00
Attorney: Kassly, Weihl & Bone
File No.: K-485514 Williams
Cause No.: 68-8464 Circuit Court St. Clair County
Summary: Date of Accident: 3/31/1968. 12:15 PM, E. St. Louis. Intersection 26th and Missouri. Defendant, east on Missouri, collided with Plaintiff north on 26th Street.

BARBOUR, ROBERT M. v S.M. WILSON & CO., et al
(Maryland Casualty)
Amount of Suit: $250,000.00
Attorney: Joseph Cohn
File No.:   Swanston
Cause No.:   68-L-394 CircuitCourt Madison County
Summary: Date of Accident: 4/24/1967. Scaffold Act suit - Granite City Steel Co.

BERRY, HAROLD W., et al v NEW MEMPHIS SAND & GRAVEL CO.
(Security)
Amount of Suit: $9,000.00
Attorney: Wagner, Conner, et al
File No.:   1-01-33023 Atkins
Cause No.:   68-9647 Circuit Court St. Clair County
Summary: Date of Accident: 1/29 & 1/30/1968. Defendant, intalling sewer for Town of Centrevile. Plaintiff claims Defendant trespassed on Plaintiff's property.

BAUCOM, BERNICE v KANASKE, EVELENA (Security Insurance) (See also Mossier)
Amount of Suit: $15,000.00
Attorney: Vic Mosele
File No.:   8-25-5660 Atkins
Cause No.:   66-L-720 CircuitCourt Madison County
Summary: Date of Accident: 1/16/1966. 12:45 AM, Rt. 40, St. Clair County. Plaintiff, a passenger of Defendant, traveling west on Rt. 40, lost control of auto and crossed on the wrong side and collided with auto by eastbound Cato. Wanton and willful case by Plaintiff.

OWENS, CHAS. v NEW YORK CENTRAL RAILROAD
Amount of Suit: $750,000.00
Attorney: O'Connell & Waller
File No.: 7-24326 Olson
Cause No.: 66-4639 Circuit Court St. Clair County
Summary: Date of Accident: 4/23/1966. New York Central Transport Yards in E. St. Louis, IL. Plaintiff, employed as a truck driver by the New York Central Transport Co., in connection with piggy-back operation. Plaintiff claims that around 3:00 PM a semi-trailer fell on him because railroad car was in defective condition.

WILKINSON, ELSIE, etc. v ULLMAN, WALTER, et al
(Maryland Casualty)
Amount of Suit: Count I - $30,000.00; Count II - $50,000.00
Attorney: Dudley Sullivan
File No.: 560-A-20505 Marshall
Cause No.: 66-3381 Circuit Court St. Clair County
Set for Trial: 11/13/1966
Summary: Date of Accident: 10/15/1965. Rt. 40 near Highland. Five car collision – all automobiles inolved are named as parties to this lawsuit.

COX, RUBEN G. v ALTON & SOUTHERN RAILROAD COMPANY
Amount of Suit: $100,000.00
Attorney: Dreman & Sterling
File No.: Foley
Cause No.: 66-4099 Circuit Court St. Clair County
Set for Trial: 12/11/1966
Summary: Date of Accident: 8/26/1964. FELA Case. 11:05 at oil house at Alton & Southern. Plaintiff and fellow employee lifting oil drum when he felt pain in back.

CONTINENTAL INSURANCE CO. v LIBERTY MUTUAL INSURANCE CO.
Amount of Suit: $6,400.00
File No.:   46 AL 19260 Gordon
Summary: Date of Accident: 1/23/1964. Wesbrook, employed by Granite City Steel Co., injured while loading trailer transported to Company by Bowler. Bowler insured by Continental who paid Wesbrook $6,400. Trailer insured by Liberty Mutual who refused to pay. This is Plaintiff suit to recover payment made by Continental.

McLEAN, DONALD, Admr. v ANDREWS, OPAL (Commercial Union Insurance Group)
Amount of Suit: $75,000.00
Attorney: Vic Mosele
File No.:   46-14512-1 McWilliams
Cause No.:   67-L-164 CircuitCourt Madison County
Summary: Date of Accident: 1/29/1966. Wrongful death action. 10:00 AM, assured's apartment building, 254 Main Street, Venice, IL. Deceased, a tenant of Defendant, asphyxiated in his room.

DOWDY, DONALD LEE, et al v KARNIGIS, NICK (Hartford)
Amount of Suit: Count I - $10,000.00; Count II - $2,500.00
Attorney: C.E. Heiligenstein
File No.:   46-L-18608 Tegtmeier
Cause No.:   68-8669 Circuit Court St. Clair County
Summary: Date of Accident: 4/2/1967. 7:55 PM. Plaintiff, a customer at Defendant's Bowlarama at 6100 Collinsville Road, E. St. Louis, IL, scuffling with other boys fell into broken plate glass window and cut self. Plaintiff demanded $4,000 - Defendant offered $750.

GLEASON, WILBUR H. v ALTON COMMUNITY UNIT SCHOOL DISTRICT, et al (Security)
Amount of Suit: $12,500.00
Attorney: Wiseman, Hallett, et al
File No.:   1-01-33405 Atkins
Cause No.:   68-L-112 CircuitCourt Madison County
Summary: Date of Accident: 12/31/1967. Before noon at Haskell Park, 12th & Liberty Streets, Alton, IL. Plaintiff was riding on sled with other boys and adult and was struck and injured by sled of third person.

BATTOE, EMILY v FRIDAY, JOE et al d/b/a Lake Christine (Security)
Amount of Suit: $17,500.00
Attorney: Sprague, Sprague & LeChien
File No.:   1-01-25224 Atkins
Cause No.:   68-8217 Circuit Court St. Clair County
Summary: Date of Accident: 5/9/1967. At Defendant's Lake Christine. Plaintiff, fishing at lake, stumbled over log which had fallen onto pathway.

REEVES, IRVIN v NORFOLK & WESTERN RAILWAY CO.
Amount of Suit: $100,000.00
Attorney: Morris B. Chapman
File No.:   161-3764 Sample
Cause No.:   68-8361 Circuit Court St. Clair County
Summary: Date of Accident: 9/16/1967. FELA Case, Madison Yards. Plaintiff, a carman, slipped on step while dismounting from railroad car.

McGUIRE, JOHN F. v THE MONSANTO COMPANY, et al
(Hartford)
Amount of Suit: $110,000.00
Attorney: Wagner, Conner, et al
File No.:   46-L-28239/ 46-C-25096 Dunn
Cause No.:   68-190 District Court, E. St. Louis
Summary: Date of Accident: 8/27/1968. Scaffold Act case. 2:00 PM, Monsanto Co., Sauget, IL. Plaintiff, an empoloyee of the Corrigan Co., fell about 30 feet from pipes on which he was working.

EUBANKS, FERn & L.W. v VILLAGE OF DUPO, ILLINOIS
(Hartford)
Amount of Suit: Haley, Bardgett & Williamson
Attorney: 875-7500
File No.:   68-8372 Circuit Court St. Clair County
Summary: Date of Accident: 6/27/1967. Plaintiff's house on State Rt. 3, Dupo, IL. Plaintiff's claim there was an explosion and fire at their house as a result of a gas leak from the gaslines owned and operated by Defendant.

BYRD, DEXTER L., a minor v EAST ST. LOUIS SCHOOL DISTRICT 189
(Continental)
Amount of Suit: Count I - $10,000.00; Count II - $300.00
Attorney: Massa and Williams
File No.:   46 GL 46287 Gerding
Cause No.:   68-8195 Circuit Court St. Clair County
Summary: Date of Accident: 1/19/1968. 2:05 M at Hughes-Quinn School, E. St. Louis, IL. 14 year old Plaintiff, thrown down stairway by Co-Defendant physical education teacher.

REESE, RAYMOND, et al v MISSOURI PACIFIC TRUCK LINES, INC., et al
(Hartford)
Amount of Suit: Count I- $50,000.00; Count II - $1,000.00;
Count III - $10,000.00; Count IV - $10,000.00
Attorney: James McRoberts
File No.: 46 KAL 26909 Yoakam
Cause No.: USDC, East St. Louis
Summary: Date of Accident: 11/1/1968. Rt. 3, Brooklyn, IL. Defendant, north and Plaintiff's, south, followed by Co-Defendant, Raining. Plaintiff's skidded across highway and collided with Defendant after which Co-Defendant collided with Plaintiff.

TAYLOR, GEORGE v MESTA-WILSON FOSTER, et al
(Commerical Union)
Amount of Suit: $250,000.00
Attorney: John D. Hayes
File No.: Harring
Cause No.: 68-I-18384 Circuit Court, Cook County
Summary: Scaffold Act case. We are local counsel for purpose of attending the deposition of F.J. Miller of Mesta-Wilson-Foster

SELPH, GLADYS v MADISON COUNTY MUTUAL AUTOMOBILE INSURANCE CO.
Attorney: James Bandy
File No.: J W Knox
Summary: Date of Accident: 4/9/1967. Uninsured motorists claim. 2;30 AM, Illinois Rt. 203 near Bend Road in Madison County, IL. Assured's northbound auto struck an abandoned car.

MOSIER, FRANKLIN L. v KANASKE, EVALINA
(Security) (See also Baucom v Kanaske)
Amount of Suit: $100,000.00
Attorney: Massa and Williams
File No.: 8-25-56600 Atkins
Cause No.: 68-7833 Circuit Court St. Clair County
Summary: Date of Accident: 1/16/1966. 12:45 AM at Rt. 40, St. Clair County. Plaintiff, a passenger of Defendant traveling west on Rt. 40, lost control of auto and crossed over on the wrong side and collided with by eastbound auto. This is a passenger wanton and wilful case.

YORK, III, CLARENCE THOMAS, a minor v COMMUNITY UNIFIED SCHOOL DISTRICT #9
Attorney: Callis, Filcoff, Brandt & Gitchoff
File No.: Continental Insurance Co. - Mr. Jerry J. Ward
Cause No.: 68-22 CircuitCourt Madison County
Summary: Date of Accident: 1/8/1968. Minor Plaintiff is gravely ill. Notice of Petition to take Deposition for Purpose of Perpetuating Testimony filed 1/8/68. Plaintiff deposition taken 1/15 re allegations his injuries and condition due to fall on playground at McKinley School.

LANGE, EDWIN W. v TERMINAL RAILROAD ASSN., et al
(Hartford)
Amount of Suit: $100,000.00
Attorney: Strawn, Kinder & Talbert
File No.: 46-KAL 17436 Yoakam
Cause No.: 68-7873 Circuit Court St. Clair County
Summary: Date of Accident: 4/14/1967. 2:30 PM E. St. Louis, Missouri Avenue at GM&O tracks. Plaintiff, east on Missouri, stopped at railroad crossing and rear ended by Defendtan's truck.

HARTMAN v BASSSLER v HARNETIAUX
Amount of Suit: $125,000.00
Attorney: P - Greenberg & Jansen; D Graves - Reed & Armstrong; D Basler - Meyer & Meyer
File No.: John Kelsey, Greenville, IL
Cause No.: 68-L-36 Circuit Court Bond County
Summary: Date of Accident: 7/6/1967. 2:30 PM, Atcheson Shell Service Station, Rtes. 40 & 127, Greenville, IL. 3 P D was general contractor to remodel service station. Plaintiff was employee of third P D. Plaintiff, working in bottom of excavation and claims that heavy equipment operated by Defendant's caused sides to cave in. Defendants were either employees or subcontractors of third P D.

WELLS, JAMES DEAN v Al N. AMANN & CO., et al
(Hartford)
Amount of Suit: $15,000.00
Attorney: Ray Freeark
File No.: 46-L-19818 Yoakam
Cause No.: 68-7835 Circuit Court St. Clair County
Summary: Date of Accident: 10/6/1967. 4:30 PM in front of assured's premises at 130 W. A Street, Belleville. Plaintiff slipped and fell on wooden grate in sidewalk as he was entering insured's premises. It was raining at the time.

TICE, WILLIAM T., Admr. v DRENNAN, JOHN J., et al
(Ed. Horrigan)
Summary: Date of Accident: 7/15/1967. Wrongful death action. IL Route 50, 1 1/2 miles east of Lebanon, IL. Deceased a passenger in westbound auto drive by Drennan which collided with eastbound auto driven by Haselhorst.

CASTILE, CHERYL, et al v ATLAS BUILDING MATERIAL CORP., et al (Hartford)
Amount of Suit: Count I - $25,000.00; Count II - $5,000.00; Count III - $500.00
Attorney: Kassly, Weihl & Bone
File No.: 46 Kal 20259 - Yoakam
Cause No.: 67-7644 Circuit Court St. Clair County
Summary: Date of Accident: 10/24/1967. 12:30 PM on Pocket Road near Adams in Centreville, IL. Defendant, north on Pocket Road and Plaintiff's south. Plaintiff's crossed centerline and hit Defendant head on.

MUSSKOPF, KEVIN v YOUNG, L.R. CONSTRUCTION CO., et al (Hartford)
Amount of Suit: Count I - $50,000.00; Count II - $10,000.00
Attorney: Jerome Lopinot
File No.: HO 150 L 49805 Jamison
Cause No.: CIV 67-7198 Circuit Court St. Clair County
Summary: Date of Accident: 9/2/1967. 2:55 PM at Highway 157 & 3 in Cahokia, IL. Defendant, digging ditch for installation of pipe lines. Plaintiff, digging tunnel in ditch and it caved in on him.

LITTLEFIELD, EUGENE v ALTON & SOUTHERN
Attorney: Paul Waller
File No.: Fiket
Summary: Date of Accident: 12/21/62. FELA case. Plaintiff Foreman, hit his head on top of doorway to engine as he was getting in and now has detached retina of right eye.

McDONALD, JAMES v W.L. WAGGONER TRUCK CO. & James M. Armer
(Hartford)
Amount of Suit: $35,000.00
Attorney: Neville & Rice
File No.:   HO 277 KAL 10480 Yoakam
Cause No.:   CIV 67-7346 Circuit Court St. Clair County
Set for Trial: 3/3/1967
Summary: Date of Accident: 10/13/1967. 12 Noon at subway on Broadway in E. St. Louis, IL. Defendant's truck, east on Broadway, lost control on wet pavement and skidded onto wrong side colliding with Plaintiff's westbound car.

BLACK, MABELL P. v McKEE, JAMES W.
(Continental)
Amount of Suit: $20,000.00
Attorney: LIsteman, Bandy & Hamilton
File No.:   46 AI 31983 Gerding
Cause No.:   67-7110 Circuit Court St. Clair County
Summary: Date of Accident: 8/3/1966. 9:10 PM, US 50 and Estates View Drive. Plaintiff, east on 50, stopped to make left turn into Estates View and rear ended by Defendant.

WILLIAMS, DONALD v LACLEDE STEEL COMPANY, et al
(Commercial Union)
Amount of Suit: $50,000.00
Attorney: Robert McGlynn
File No.:   46-13260 McWilliams
Cause No.:   67-7342 Circuit Court St. Clair County
Summary: Date of Accident: 5/24/1966. Plaintiff, a switchman for Terminal RR, injured on Defendant's premises at Madison, IL. Plaintiff, attempting to operate switch #3, claims switch was defective.

GROETEKA, CARL H. & CECELIA v W-R SCHILLER CONSTRUCTION CO., et al (Maryland Casualty) (See also Dunaway v W-R Schiller & Hickey v. Schiller)
Amount of Suit: Count II $100,000.00; Count VI - $75,000.00
Attorney: Carr, Raffaelle & Cook
File No.:   560-L-18100 Robert G. Matheny
Cause No.:   67-6966 Circuit Court St. Clair County
Summary: Date of Accident: 5/13/1967. IL Route 159 in St. Clair County, IL. Plaintiffs injured in three car collision claiming that dirt washed onto highway from real estate being graded by Defendant.

TELFORD, MICHELLE, et al v LITCHFIELD BITUMINOUS CO.
(Commercial Union)
Amount of Suit: Count I - $15,000.00; Count II - $15,000.00
Attorney: Meyer & Meyer
File No.:   0-110438-A McWilliams
Cause No.:   68-L-44 Circuit Court Bond County
Summary: Date of Accident: 12/4/1967. 8:00 PM, Spruce Street and Harris Avenue, Greenville, IL. Plaintiff's, traveling north on Spruce Street, struck manhole. Defendant had job of widening street and installing storm sewers.

LURTZ, STEVEN K. v ELKS WESTHAVEN, et al
(Commercial Union)
Amount of Suit: $4,500.00
Attorney: Johnson, Ducey & Feder
File No.:   46-13321-1 OBI McWIlliams
Cause No.:   CIV 67-6996 Circuit Court Belleville
Summary: Date of Accident: 6/22/1966. 4:00 PM, Westhaven Swimming Pool. Minor Plaintiff slipped and fell at edge of pool.

ROYAL, JO ANN, a minor v BERZANSKY, MYRTLE, et al
(Commercial Union)
Amount of Suit: $75,000.00
Attorney: Sprague, Sprague & LeChien
File No.: 46-13413-1 ABI McWilliams
Cause No.: 67-L-529 CircuitCourt Madison County
Summary: Date of Accident: 7/8/1966. 12:30 PM, Elm and Combs Streets, Collinsville, IL. Plaintiff, a passenger in Co-Defendant's westbound car on Elm, struck by Defendants southbound car on Combs.

HAMPTON, BETTY v ROBERTS, KENNETH
(Continental)
Amount of Suit: $15,000.00
Attorney: Jack C. Harper
File No.: 46 GL 39556 Gerding
Cause No.: 67-7591 Circuit Court St. Clair County
Summary: Date of Accident: 3/15/1967. Defendant's premises at 413 Art, State Park Place, Collinsville, IL. Plaintiff claims she stepped on wooden bridge which collapsed causing her to be injured. Plaintiff's attorneys demanded $9,000.00. Defendant's offered $750.00 plus medicals.

McDONOUGH, MARGARET v MATHIS & NOERPER
(Harlan & Harlan)
Amount of Suit: Count I - $1,050.00; Count II - $3,271.95; Count III - $9,919.01
Attorney: Floyd E. Crowder
File No.: 54295 LH Lary Harlan
Cause No.: 67 CIV 43 Circuit Court Waterloo - Monroe County

CASE, URSULA, et al v THOMPSON'S GAS, INC., et al
(Employers-Commercial Union)
Amount of Suit: Count XXV - $24,500.00;
Count XXVI - $24,500.00
Attorney: Norton & Kionka
File No.: K4-3502 McWilliams
Cause No.: 69-1493 Circuit Court St. Clair County
Summary: Date of Accident: 5/30/1969. Residence at Rt. 2, Mascoutah, IL. Plaintiff's were tenants at residence and Plaintiff, Ursula Case, attempted to light hot water heater when there was an explosion. Defendant is the gas supplier.

LAUGHLIN, JAMES, MICHAEL (Deceased) v EAST ST. LOUIS SCHOOL DISTRICT #189 (Great American Insurance Co.)
Amount of Suit: $30,000.00
Attorney: Kassly, Weihl, Carr & Bone
File No.: 365 L 3761 Sauve
Cause No.: 65-1801 Circuit Court St. Clair County
Set for Trial: 12/5/1965
Summary: Date of Accident: 10/20/1964. 10:15 AM, E. St. Louis High School. 300 pound 17 year old Plaintiff completed 600 yard run/walk physical fitness project and thereafter collapsed and died.

GIBSON, SHELBY v ASSOCIATED FURNITURE COMPANY, INC. & ROYCE FERGUSON (Hartford) (See also Dooley)
Amount of Suit: $20,000.00
Attorney: Robert F. Quinn
File No.: Tegtmeier
Cause No.: 69-L-766 CircuitCourt Madison County
Summary: Date of Accident: 9/25/1969. Rt. 143 near Wanda Road, Madison County, IL. Plaintiff, traveling west, rear ended by Defendant.

DOOLEY, SHIRLEY v. ASSOCIATED FURNITURE CO., INC. & ROYCE FERGUSON (Hartford) (See also Gibson)
Amount of Suit: $20,000.00
Attorney: Robert F. Quinn
File No.: Tegtmeier
Cause No.: 69-L-872 CircuitCourt Madison County
Summary: Date of Accident: 9/25/1969. Rt. 143 near Wanda Road, Madison County, IL. Plaintiff, a passenger in truck traveling west, rear ended by Defendant.

SHORE, HELEN v RICHARD MAURER & THOMPSON'S BOTTLE GAS, INC. (Employees Commercial Union)
Amount of Suit: $25,000.00
Attorney: Brady, Donovan & Hatch
File No.: 46-16713-1 McWilliams
Cause No.: 69-558 Circuit Court St. Clair County
Summary: Date of Accident: 10/22/1968. Rt. 50 near South Ruby Lane, St. Clair County, IL. Plaintiff, traveling east on Rt. 50, stopped for school children and was rear ended by Defendant.

HAVEN, RICHARD, a minor v WALTER, WILLIAM, et al (Commerical Union)
Attorney: Irving Wiseman
File No.: 60-H-10671-1 Witte
Cause No.: 3293 Ciry Court Alton, IL
Summary: Date of Accident: 10/19/1962. 834 Chouteau, Godfrey, IL. Five year old Plaintiff fell off swing set at Defendant's yard.

ENGELMAN, ROBERT, et al v GENERAL MOTORS CORPORATION et al
(Royal-Globe)
Amount of Suit:	$500,000.00
Attorney:	Richard E. White
File No.:	684-2411
Cause No.:	74-L-35-Circuit Court Jackson County, Murphysboro
Summary:	Date of Accident: 3/7/1973. 1971 Pontiac Bonneville allegedly went out of control and crashed due to defects in steering mechanism.

BENNETT, GEORGE W. v BICKEL, WILLIAM, M.D., et al
(Forrest Tozer)
File No.:	69300-006-Tozer
Cause No.:	CV77-0014-D-USDC Danville, IL

BUNTING, CHARLES v SMITH v. NATIONAL POOL EQUIPMENT CO.
(Commercial Union)
Amount of Suit:	Count I - $50,000.00, Count II - $50,000.00
Attorney:	P. Tom Meyer and Carl Runge,
	3P - Allen Churchill (Town & Country Motel)
File No.:	W2-1411 Wilde
Cause No.:	CIV 4958 USDC Southern Dist.
Summary:	Date of Accident: 6/13/1970. Plaintiff was a guest at Co-Defendants motel in Arkansas and he claims that he slipped and fell from a diving board. Co-Defendant brought a 3rd party suit against our client that sold the diving board.

VAUGHN, DONALD, Admr., etc. v EISELE, OWEN J., M.D.
(Commercial Union)
Amount of Suit: $150,000.00
Attorney: Morris Chapman
File No.:   K4-7917 Wilde
Cause No.:   74 L 941 Circuit Court St. Clair County
Summary: Date of Accident: 3/14/1973. 8:20 o'clock AM.
Defendant administering anesthesia to child for operation to correct cross-eyed condition. Child died before surgery commenced.

STOBBS, WILLIAM A. v DR. BRUCE VEST, et al
(Commercial Union)
Amount of Suit: $200,000.00
Attorney: Cohn, Carr, Korein, Kunin and Brennan (Runge)
File No.:   Wilde
Cause No.:   75-I-639 Circuit Court Madison County
Summary: Date of Accident: 4/25/1973. Medical malpractice case.
Plaintiff in auto accident 4/25/73 and admitted to St. Joseph's Hospital at Alton until 5/14/73. Defendant is radiologist. Plaintiff claims that fractured cervical vertebra not discovered and this is basis for his suit.

GIBBAR, BEATRICE v DENNIS M. PREUHSNER and DALEE OIL CO.
Amount of Suit: $35,000.00
Attorney: Ducey and Feder
File No.:   32-2200 Gates
Cause No.:   75 L 1750 Circuit Court St. Clair County
Summary: Date of Accident: 7/11/1973. Rt. 159 at Douglas Road - intersection collision

SMITH, CHRISTINE, et al v EAST ST. LOUIS AND INTERURBAN WATER COMPANY (Royal Globe)
Amount of Suit: Count I - $15,000.00, Count II - $7,500.00
Attorney: Goldenhersh and Goldenhersh
File No.: XP 653A26309 - Langhammer
Cause No.: 74 L 3226, Circuit Court St. Clair County
Summary: Date of Accident: 2/19/1973. 8:15 AM in front of 1511 Lynch, E. St. Louis, IL. Defendants fire hydrant was knocked over by another automobile and water ran onto pavement and froze. Thereafter Plaintiff's automobile slid on ice and collided with another automobile, etc.

HUNTER v PARKE-DAVIS & ENRIQUE RODREQUES (Commercial Union)
Amount of Suit: $100,000.00
Attorney: Talbert
Cause No.: ED 73 L 311
Summary: Date of Accident: 5/15/1970. Anesthetic agent of "Katalar" used – supposedly caused brain damage

ROSENE, ALFRED, III v.GENERAL MOTORS, et al (Royal Globe)
Amount of Suit: $15,000.00
Attorney: Robert McGlynn
File No.: R653A-25721-English
Cause No.: 73 L 2193, Circuit Court St. Clair County
Summary: Date of Accident: 12/19/1972. FELA action against terminal RR and negligence action against GM. 10:40 PM on GM property in St. Louis. Plaintiff, a switchman for Terminal, injured because of alleged close clearance at dock due to rack of GM being too close to tracks.

GRISHAM, MARLYS K., v SKASOL Corporation, et al
(Northwestern National)
Amount of Suit: $50,000.00
Attorney: Meyer and Meyer, Greenville
File No.: 29-6680-Brown
Cause No.: 74 L 3, Cir Ct. Bond County, Greenville, IL
Summary: Date of Accident: 9/24/1972. Products Liability case. Plaintiff, an employee of Hillsboro Hospital, opened cabinet when bottle of "Plunger" manufactuerd by Defendant fell from shelf and broke. Plaintiff sustained burns.

SPARLING, JUDITH v PEABODY COAL COMPANY, et al
(Continental)
Amount of Suit: $1,000,000.00
Attorney: Carr, Rafaelle and Cook
File No.: 46 GL 53407 - Gerding
Cause No.: 68-9797, Circuit Court St. Clair County
Summary: Date of Accident: 9/11/1953. Perry County, IL. Plaintiff's father purchased real estate from Defendant's predecessor on 4/24/47. Over 5 years later on 9/11/53, Plaintiff injured while playing on slag mound.

SMITH, MICHAEL v SHELL OIL & COMBUSTION ENGINEerING v. INSECO, Inc. (Commercial Union)
Amount of Suit: $300,000.00
Attorney: P-McGrady, Madden & McGrady - Gillespie; Shell-Gordon Broom; Combution-Howard Bowman
File No.: K4-10258 - Hoerath
Cause No.: A-CIV-74-26 USDC Souther District of Illinois
Summary: Date of Accident: 11/12/1973. Scaffold Act case. P, employee of Inesco, which had contracted to do work at Shell Oil in Wood River. Shell and Combustion bring indemnity action

DECKARD, DENNIS v. DR. DOY FREELAND, et al
(Commercial Union)
Amount of Suit: $100,000.00
Attorney: Jack Norton
File No.: K4-8956 Wilde
Cause No.: 74-L-1965, Circuit Court St. Clair County
Summary: Date of Accident: 6/5/1972. Malpractice case. P injured while riding motorcycle which collided with automobile. P suffered a fractured right leg (fibula and tibia) lacerations of the skull and fractured right metacarpal index finger.

WALLACE, MARJORIE v. ALAN SKIRBALL, M.D.
(Commercial Union)
Amount of Suit: $250,000.00
Attorney: Meyer and Kaucher
File No.: 74-L-494, Circuit Court Madison County
Summary: Date of Accident: 9/7/1972. Medical malpractice case. Defendant performed labarotomy on Plaintiff and during course of surgery, inadvertently lacerated colon.

NORTON, CHARLES v. SHELL OIL COMPANY v. INSECO, INC.
(Commercial Union)
Amount of Suit: $425,000.00
Attorney: Karnes, Starnes, Nester & Stegmeyer
File No.: K4-7184-Hoerath
Cause No.: 74-L-563, Circuit Court Madison County
Summary: Date of Accident: 8/31/1973. Scaffold Act case. P, employee of Inesco, which had contracted to do work at Shell Oil in Wood River. P fell from a support or something else and was injured. Shell brings indemnity action

MARTIN, ROBERT v. TERMINAL RAILROAD ASSN. v. CITY PRODUCTS
(Royal Globe)
Amount of Suit: $30,000.00
Attorney: P-Ed Brennan; Terminal RR-Dick Boyle
File No.:   A653A-21930 Temple
Cause No.:   71-1157, Circuit Court St. Clair County
Summary: Date of Accident: 4/18/1970. FELA indemnity action. At CD Yards of Terminal RR. P, a switchman, fell.

CREASON, EARL, et al v. GENERAL MOTORS CORPORATION
(Royal Globe)
Amount of Suit: $25,000.00
Attorney: C.E. Heiligenstein
File No.:   R6-91A-09390 F.F. Koehler, Springfield, IL
Cause No.:   73 L 112, Circuit Court St. Clair County
Summary: Date of Accident: 2/17/1971. Premises of GM, Danville, IL. Plaintiffs were employees of a subcontractor and were injured when some beams fell on them.

JOHNSON, RONALD, et al v. GENERAL MOTORS CORP., et al
(Royal Globe)
Amount of Suit: $75,000.00
Attorney: Meyer and Meyer, Greenville
File No.:   R635A-24391 English
Cause No.:   71-136, Cir Ct. Montgomery County (Hillsboro)
Summary: Products Liability case. Automobile collision at Montgomery and Ryder Sts. in Litchfield, IL. Plaintiff east on Ryder and Co-Defendant driving 1970 Chevrolet Chevelle south on Montogmery. Plaintiff claims motor mount failure caused throttle to stick.

HENDRICKS, ARNOLD R. v. WHITE MOTOR CORPORATION v. DETROIT DIESEL, a Division of GENERAL MOTORS CORPORATION (Royal Globe)
Amount of Suit: $500,000.00
Attorney: P - Rex Carr, White Motor - Bob Schmieder
Cause No.:   74-130E, USDC E. St. Louis
Summary: Date of Accident: 6/12/1972. Plaintiff Driving White Motor tractor claims accelerator stuck. White Motors claims accelerator assembly manufactured and furnished by GM.

RODGERS, GEORGE v. GENERAL TIRE v. KOHL INDUSTRIES v. K.S.M. CORPORATION (Commercial Union)
Amount of Suit: $250,000.00
Attorney: P Heiligenstein, Kohl-John O'Connell
File No.:   David Rowland
Cause No.:   73 II 3080, Circuit Court St. Clair County
Summary: Date of Accident: 4/23/1973. Scaffold Act case. Monday, 1:25 PM. Plaintiff, a sheet metal worker, employed by Kohl, backed off roof of General Tire at Mt. Vernon, IL while installing roof decking. Defendant's sue Kohl for indemnity who sues KSM for indemnity.

ZANDER, LESLIE v. JOHN DEERE COMPANY
Amount of Suit: $150,000.00
Attorney: Listeman, Bandy and Hamilton
File No.:   John Hayes
Cause No.:   74 L 886, Cir Ct. St. Clair County
Summary: Date of Accident: 6/13/1973. Products Liability case involving John Deere Model 55 Combine. Plaintiff got pant leg caught in sprocket chain injuring left leg.

PARMLEY, DONALD v. TOM CASAVELY FORD, INC. & RICHARD DUSKY (Northwestern National)
Amount of Suit: $15,000.00
Attorney: Chapman & Chapman (Gary Peel)
File No.: 29-7693 Mary Robertson
Cause No.: 75 LM 765, Circuit Court Madison County
Summary: Date of Accident: 8/31/1975. 1:55 AM, Rt. 66 at Highway 111, Madison County, IL. Plaintiff, westbound on Rt. 66, rearended by Defendant.

SPEARMAN, TULSIA v. THOMAS E. SLOVER and THOMECZEK OIL COMPANY (Northwestern National)
Amount of Suit: $7,500.00
Attorney: Goldenhersh and Goldenhersh
File No.: 32-2097 Brown (Gates)
Cause No.: 74 LM 2894
Summary: Date of Accident: 1/29/1973. Friday, 6:55 AM intersection Rt. 3 and 8th Sts., Sauget, IL. Defendant north on Rt. 3 struck by Plaintiff's westbound car on Sotuh 8th St.

SPEARMAN, CHARLES v. CLARK OIL & SAVERSON v. GENERAL EQUIPMENT COMPANY
Amount of Suit: $38,945.72
Attorney: P-Jack Norton, Clark Oil & Saverson-Gundlach, Lee, etc., Brady Donovan, Etc.-Geo. Grove Plbm.
File No.: Wilde
Cause No.: 74 L 1350, Circuit Court St. Clair County
Summary: Date of Accident: 12/23/1973. At service station at 68th & State Sts., E. St. Louis, IL. Plaintiff claims he was a business invitee at service station and he fell into an excavation.

HEATHERLY v. CLARK OIL
(Royal Globe)
Amount of Suit: $250,000.00
Attorney: Schooley
File No.: Royal R653A20837
Cause No.: ED 71-15
Summary: Date of Accident: 6/12/1970. Plaintiff an employee of Foster Wheeler, a contractor of Clark, was loading steel, steel shifted killing Plaintiff.

REED, MARY, Admr., etc. v. SLOVER, THOMAS E. AND THOMECZEK OIL COMPANY (Northwestern National)
Amount of Suit: $100,000.00
Attorney: Goldenhersh and Goldenhersh
File No.: 32-2097 Brown
Cause No.: 74 L 2870, Circuit Court St. Clair County
Summary: Date of Accident: 1/29/1973. Wrongful death case. Friday 6:55 AM, initersection Rt. 3 and 8th Sts., Sauget, IL. Defendant north on Rt. 3 struck by Plaintiff's westbound car on South 8th St.

MUFFO, CARMEN C., etc. v. BARNES HOSPITAL, et al
(Underwriters)
Amount of Suit: $1,000,000.00
Attorney: William Gagen
File No.: 046-3 C9996 Goedde
Cause No.: 74 L 2714, Circuit Court St. Clair County
Summary: Malpractice case. Plaintiff suffers neuropathy due to taking Apresoline prescribed by Barnes Hospital Clinic from 12/72 to 2/73. Plaintiff refiled in St. Louis.

BAILEY, CLIFTON GREG v. SUNDERLAND MOTOR COMPANY INC. & GENERAL MOTORS CORP. (Royal Globe)
Amount of Suit: $250,000.00
Attorney: Wiseman, Shaigewitz and McGivern,
Co-D-Ed Moorman
File No.: 653A-24805
Cause No.: 72 L 459, Circuit Court Madison County
Summary: Date of Accident: 6/28/1970. Products Liability case. Plaintiff operating 1969 Chevrolet Camero when he struck bridge on Rt. 96 in Calhoun County, IL. Plaintiff claims motor mount defect.

BEAVERS, WILLIAMN v. TEREX, a Division of General Motors Corporation (Royal Globe)
Amount of Suit: $10,000.00
Attorney: Richard Shaikewitz
File No.: 2P653A29862 Temple
Cause No.: 74 LM 51, Circuit Court Madison County
Summary: Date of Accident: 1/25/1972. Plaintiff Operating C6 Euclid Dozer. Dozer did not have heater. Plaintiff claims he started to get out of dozer to warm his hands and slipped and injured himself.

ERVIN, JOHN v. SEARS, ROEBUCK v. FLAGG-UTICA CORP. (American Mutual Liability Co.)
Amount of Suit: $500,000.00
Attorney: Wiseman, Hallett, Mosele and Keehner
File No.: CGA 7181-B-257-205385 Hoefle
Cause No.: 64-R-114 7, Circuit Court Madison County
Set for Trial: November 27
Summary: Date of Accident: 1/30/1963. Omaha, NE. Plaintiff purchased insulated underwear from Sears Roebuck and it caught fire while Plaintiff was welding. Sears seeks indemnity from Flagg-Utica Corp.

KOCH, ROY v. REICHERT GRAIN COMPANY, INC. et al
(Commercial Union)
Amount of Suit: $1,000,000.00
Attorney: LeChien and Hantla
File No.:   Wilde
Cause No.:   74 L 3104, Circuit Court St. Clair County
Summary: Date of Accident: 1/25/1973. At Defendant's buisness at 600 S. 1st St., Belleville, IL. Plaintiff, an employee, sustained an electrical burn while engaged in his employement necessitating the amputation of his right leg below the knee.

LEAHY, RICHARD v. C.D. PETERS CONSTRUCTION Co., et al
(Northwestern National)
Amount of Suit: $25,000.00
Attorney: Callis, Schooley, Filcoff and Hartman
File No.:   82-2896 Helbling
Cause No.:   76 L 22, Circuit Court Madison County
Summary: Date of Accident: 6/1/1975. Scaffold Act case.

RUSSELL, CHARLES J. v. NORFOLK AND WESTERN RAILWAY CO.
Amount of Suit: $225,000.00
Attorney: Haley, Frederickson, Stubbs and Abele
File No.:   Lawsuit 161-4785 (L-12861) Sample
Cause No.:   73 L 2916, Circuit Court St. Clair County
Summary: Date of Accident: 1/21/1973. FELA case. 10:30 AM Plaintiff, a switchman riding on side of car, came in contact with car on adjacent track.

ULMER, LORETTA v. HOPKINS OIL COMPANY, et al
(Northwestern National)
Amount of Suit: $1,250,000.00
Attorney: Jack Norton
File No.:   32-2549-D Brown
Cause No.:   76 L 3102, Circuit Court St. Clair County
Summary: Date of Accident: 2/18/1975. 2:10 PM on US Rt. 40 near Keyesport Road in Bond County, IL. Defendant west on Rt. 40 and Plaintiff east, when Defendant made left turn in front of Plaintiffs.

FOLEY, JOHN J., JR. v. WRIGHT, H.H. Co., et al
(Royal Globe)
Amount of Suit: $75,000.00
Attorney: O'Connell and Waller
File No.:   6P653A-40797 Langhammer
Cause No.:   75 L 3170, Circuit Court St. Clair County
Summary: Date of Accident: 4/21/1974. Structural Work Act case. Defendant. leased crane and operator to Wilbur Waggoner. Crane operator dropped piping on Plaintiff.

RIESS, GELINDO J. v. COACHMAN OIL COMPANY
(Northwestern National)
Amount of Suit: $25,000.00
Attorney: Mateyka and Hill
File No.:   32-2627 Brown
Cause No.:   75 L 437, Circuit Court Madison County
Summary: Date of Accident: 1/1/1974. Fall down case. Plaintiff slipped and fell on ice at Defendant's premises at 1151 Edwardsville Rd, Granite City, IL.

PULLY, EARL T., v. HERTZ, et al
(Royal Globe)
Amount of Suit: $40,000.00
Attorney: Thomas Lakin
File No.: R653A-23999 Temple
Cause No.: 73 L 001065, St. Clair County
Summary: Date of Accident: 4/10/1972. Plaintiff rented 1981 Ford 10-passenger station wagon from Hertz on 4/7/1972. At time of accdient Plaintiff was a passenger and Defendant Rucker was driving. 7:20 PM on 1-70 near I-57 in Effingham County, IL, 10 occupants in station wagon. Right front tire blew out causing car to leave highway.

ALFARO, BETTY JANE and ELVIE DEE ALFARO v. MANOR BAKING COMPANY, a Corp., FIRESTONE TIRE AND RUBBER Co., a Corp., SAYRE AND FISHER COMPANIES, INC., KENNETH HARTBARGER and WHITE MOTOR COMPANY, A corp.
Amount of Suit: Counts 1, 3, 5 & 7 - $50,000.00;
Counts 2,4 & 6 - $25,000.00
Attorney: Gordon Nielson
File No.: Royal Globe #XR653A24719
Cause No.: 74 L 511, Madison County
Summary: Date of Accident: 8/12/1972. Manor driving tractor trailer east on 270 – blew right front tie, into trailer park.

PAYRCE, CHAS v. KRAMER, C.E., M.D.
(Commercial Union)
Amount of Suit: $50,000.00
Attorney: Paul Storment
File No.: Wilde
Cause No.: 73 L 2856, Circuit Court Belle
Summary: Date of Accident: 10/20/1972. Malpractice Case. Plaintiff went to Defendant with sore middle finger on left hand. Part of finger later amputated due to staph infection. Plaintiff claims Defendant failed to properly diagnose.

PALMIER, TERRI, a minor, v. HAYS, CARLA, et al
(Royal Globe)
Amount of Suit: $50,000.00
Attorney: Terry Peebles
File No.:   9P653A-37991 Wisdom
Cause No.:   75 L 2299, Circuit Court St. Clair County
Summary: Date of Accident: 4/10/1975. 6:30 PM, intersection of Rt. 3 and Water St. in Cahokia, IL. Defendant southbound on Rt. 3 struck by Co-Defendant westbound on Water St. forcing Defendant into Plaintiff who was a pedestrian on east shoulder of Rt. 3.

AVITTS, GILBERT C. v. GENERAL MOTORS CORPORATION, et al
(Royal Globe)
Amount of Suit: $75,000.00
Attorney: Chapman & Chapman (O'Leary)
Cause No.:   74 L 719, Circuit Court Madison County
Summary: Date of Accident: 10/18/1974. GM Chevrolet Assembly Plant, St. Louis. Plaintiff, employed by Terminal RR, claims he injured himself while attempting to throw a switch.

KEHRER, MILBURN v. S.J. GROVES & SONS
(Commercial Union)
Amount of Suit: $32,859.76
Attorney: O'Connell and Waller
File No.:   Wilde
Cause No.:   75 L 3074, Circuit Court St. Clair County
Summary: Date of Accident: 11/14/1974. On Rt. 55 near Rt. 4 at Liviingston, IL. Defendant engaged in repairing highway. Plaintiff drove truck into "spreader box" operated by Defendant and Defendant crushed Plaintiff's truck between motor grader and truck.

TURNBOW, RONALD v. TERRY GILL
(Commercial Union)
Amount of Suit: $50,000.00
Attorney: Dixon, Starnes, Nexter and McDonnell
File No.:   WG 14098 Rowland
Cause No.:   76 L 2877, Circuit Court St. Clair County
Summary: Date of Accident: 5/19/1976. 3:29 PM, Defendant west and Plaintiff east on Rt. 157. Defendant made left turn in front of Plaintiff onto Triple Lakes Rd. resulting in collision.

OWENS, CRYSTAL v. PEABODY COAL COMPANY
(Old Republic Companies)
Amount of Suit: $1,000,000.00
Attorney: Paul Storment
File No.:   Perkins
Cause No.:   76 L 2013, Circuit Court St. Clair County
Summary: Date of Accident: 6/22/1975. 3:30 PM at Old Seminole Strip Pit Pond near New Athens, IL. Plaintiff jumped from cliff into pond and struck rock ledge.

DINES, LARRY v. KRAFTCO, CORPORATION, et al
(Ideal Mutual Insurance Co.)
Amount of Suit: $125,000.00
Attorney: C.E. Heiligenstein
File No.:   GL690 253 - Harold Jensen, Champaign, IL
Cause No.:   CIV 70-3840 Circuit Court St. Clair County
Summary: Date of Accident: 12/8/1969. 10:40 AM at Humko plant of Kraftco, Champaign, IL. Plaintiff, a business invitee, crosing railroad track and struck by railroad car.

BAKER, GEORGE P. (Penn Central) v GM&O
Amount of Suit: $98,000.00
Attorney: Walker & Williams
File No.: PI-36219 - Johnston
Cause No.: 72-72 U.S. District Court East St. Louis
Summary: Date of Accident: 2/4/1970. Indemnity action by Penn Central to recover $98,000.00 paid to its employee under FELA case. 9:00 am Plaintiff's employee, Robert Ballard, attempting to throw No. 2 switch in Wann Yard near Wood River, Il, injured back. Switch jointly owned by Penn Central and GM&O with written agreement that Penn Central will maintain.

BAKER, THEODORE v GUTHRIE, HOOVER, dba HOOVER'S AUTO BODY (Northwestern National)
Amount of Suit: $4,500.00
Attorney: Robert A. Hayes
File No.: 29-5094 - Brown
Cause No.: 73-LM 2256 Circuit Court St. Clair County
Summary: Date of Accident: 3/1/1973. Bailment and subrogation claim. Plaintiff delivered his '71 Cadillac to Defendant for repairs. While in Defendants possesion, automobile was stolen.

BARBER, GEORGIA, ADMR. v COHN, ARNOLD
(Hartford)
Amount of Suit: $30,000.00
Attorney: Kassley Wiehl and Bone (Becker)
File No.: 46 I 35902 - Tegtmeier
Cause No.: 70-3050 Circuit Court St. Clair County
Summary: Date of Accident: 7/6/1969. 12:30 PM, 1801 Brinson Dr., Washington Park, IL. Plaintiff's 5 year old deceased fell into cesspool and was killed.

GOOCH, HENRY v SUNNY SHIELDS MUSIC, INC.
(Great American Insurance)
Amount of Suit: $9,500.00
Attorney: Listeman, Bandy and Hamilton (Gomric)
File No.: 365-AI 8856 - Martin
Cause No.: CIV 70-2995 St. Clair County
Summary: Date of Accident: 2/11/1962. 9:20 AM Route 460 at 4100 Missouri Avenue in Alorton, IL. Plaintiff traveling east intending to turn left into Fina Station, rearended by Defendatn

CRUM & FORSTER INSURANCE COMPANIES v NORFOLK AND WESTERN et al (See also: Jones, William v. N&W)
Attorney: Heyl, Royster, Voelker and Allen
File No.: 161-4707 - Sample
Cause No.: 578-73 Circuit Court Sangamon County, IL
Summary: Declaratory judgment action by insurance carriers for Co-Defendant Coons in cast styled Wm. Jones v. N&W and Coons

DAVES, MILTON v LEON F. STREIF, et al
(Underwriters)
Amount of Suit: $42,500.00
Attorney: Meyer and Meyer (Kaucher)
File No.: 46 AI 96345 - Gerding
Cause No.: 71-2981 Circuit Court St. Clair County
Summary: Date of Accident: 4/2/1971. 8:30 AM at Douglas School, Belleville. Mentally retarded Plaintiff being transferred from one of Defendant's school buses to another injured when he ran into open bus door. Second accident on 5/14/71 at 8:30 AM at Scott Air Force Base at alley. Defendant's southbound bus stopped at curb in front of mentally retarded Plaintiff to pick him up. Plaintiff ran around to left side of bus and was struck by Co-Defendant's northbound automobile.

EPPERSON, GEORGE v NORFOLK & WESTERN RY. CO.
Amount of Suit: $100,000.00
Attorney: Chapman, Talbert and Chapman
File No.: 161-4458 - L- 12455 - Sample
Cause No.: 72-L-118 Madison County
Summary: Date of Accident: 10/8/1971. FELA case. Plaintiff, a brakeman seated in caboose, when caboose was suddenly and unexpectedly moved by impact of second engine connection cut off cars at Defendant's Madison Yards.

HAYWOOD, THOMAS, et al v WIESE, FLOYD
(Commercial Union)
Amount of Suit: I-$17,500.00; II-$17,500.00; III-$500.00
Attorney: Sprague, John, Jr.
File No.: K4-4380 - McWilliams
Cause No.: 73 L 966 Circuit Court St. Clair County
Summary: Date of Accident: 10/25/1971. 46th Street at Freedom Drive in Belleville, IL. Plaintiff east on 46th Street and Defendant west – vehicles collided.

HAHN, FRANK v NORFOLK AND WESTERN RAILWAY CO.
(Two Suits)
Amount of Suit: $50,000.00
Attorney: Talbert and Chapman
File No.: 161-4473 - Sample
Cause No.: 72-L-242 Circuit Court St. Clair County
Summary: Date of Accident: 1/21/1971. FELA Case. 8:45 AM at repair track in Madison, IL. Plaintiff was tightening train line on box car when wrench slipped causing him to hit his hand. Plaintiff demanded $40,000.00. Defendant offered $10,000.00

JONES, WILLIAM v NORFOLK AND WESTERN, et al
Amount of Suit: $250,000.00
Attorney: Ryan and Heller
File No.: L-12560 - Sample
Cause No.: 72-L-497 Circuit Court St. Clair County
Summary: Date of Accident: 9/1/1970. Coles County, IL. Plaintiff, an employee of Co-Defendant was riding in truck pulling a hayrack. Wheels of truck became caught in rails of Defendant's tracks and as Plaintiff was assisting Co-Defenant in attempting to extricate truck the rear wheels of truck threw a piece of ballast which struck and blinded one of Plaintiff's eyes.

JUENGER, LEROY v NORFOLD AND WESTERN RAILWAY Co.
Amount of Suit: $50,000.00
Attorney: Talbert and Chapman
File No.: 161-4483 (L-12510) - Sample
Cause No.: 72-L-295 Circuit Court Madison County
Summary: Date of Accident: 2/8/1972. FELA. 6:30 PM, Madison, IL. Plaintiff, using electric jack which he claims jammed while working on TOFC car. This allegedly injured Plaintiff's left shoulder.

McCLINTOCK, MARIE v L-C HIWAY HOUSE, INC.
(Underwriters Adjusting Co.)
Amount of Suit: $25,000.00
Attorney: Cox and Bassett
File No.: 76-8-498- 46 GL 47613 - Daly
Cause No.: 69-L-211 Circuit Court Madison County
Summary: Date of Accident: 4/17/1968. 10:30 PM. Parking lot of insured's premises at Lewis & Clark Restaurant, Highway 3, East Alton, IL. Plaintiff stumbled and fell as she was crossing parking lot.

OLIVER, HAROLD v SERVICE OIL CO.
(Northwestern National Insurance Group)
Amount of Suit: $25,000.00
Attorney: James J. Massa
File No.: 32-2122 - Brown
Cause No.: 73 L 441 Circuit Court Madison County
Summary: Date of Accident: 2/17/1973. Route 157, St. Clair County, IL. Defendant north and Plaintiff south when they sideswiped.

RHOADES, M.J. v NORFOLK AND WESTERN
Amount of Suit: $500,000.00
Attorney: Freeark and Harvey
File No.: L-12819 - Sample
Cause No.: 73-L-464 Circuit Court Madison County
Summary: Date of Accident: 10/8/1971. FELA. 9:15 AM at Track Shop in Decatur, IL. Plaintiff, a machinist, was caught between a locomotive wheel and a wheel turning machine.

ROOSE, WARREN E. v PENN CENTRAL RAILROAD
Amount of Suit: $100,000.00
Attorney: Hillary Hallett
File No.: GL 64398 - Helmetag
Cause No.: 70-L-807 Circuit Court Madison County
Summary: Date of Accident: 3/17/1970. FELA case. 3:30 PM, Worcester Yard, Mitchell, IL. Plaintiff claims he inhaled fumes from passing railroad car which injured him.

SPALDING, WILBUR, v ABC ERECTORS, INC.
(Employers-Commercial Union)
Amount of Suit: $100,000.00
Attorney: Talbert and Chapman
File No.:   McWilliams
Cause No.:   71-L-61 Madision County
Summary: Date of Accident: 12/21/1970. During erection of Venture Store in Alton, Defendant was subcontracotr to erect external concrete walls and put in reinforcing steel and iron mesh into concrete. Defendant was employed by R.B. Cleveland Co. Plaintiff brings suit based on negligence and Scaffold Act.

ZAGORSKI v. ILLINOIS CENTRAL v GENERAL MOTORS
(Royal Globe)
Amount of Suit: $750,000.00
Attorney: Kassley Wiehl and Bone (Jon Carlson)
File No.:   R 653A-23131 - Heim
Cause No.:   70-3081 Circuit Court St. Clair County
Summary: Date of Accident: 1/24/1970. Grade crossing collision at Loda, IL. Train struck gasoline truck resulting in deaths of all people in lead diesel. Illinois Central sues General Motors for indemnity.

ALBERTINA, VERNA v HARRY N. ELLSWSORTH, et al
(Northwestern National Insurance Group)
Amount of Suit: $65,000.00
Attorney: James J. Massa
File No.:   82-2182 - Brown
Cause No.:   72-L-579 Circuit Court Madison County
Summary: Date of Accident: 4/28/1972. 7:40 PM. Plaintiff claims she fell on sidewalk at 15 North Clinton Street, Collinsville, IL

MARTIN, RUTH K., Executor of the Estate of Scott C. Martin, deceased v DONALD E. GILLMORE and COMMUNITY SPORTS, INC., dba Tamarack Country Club
(Royal Globe)
Amount of Suit: $100,000.00
Attorney: Ray Freeark
File No.: 7P653A28402 - Temple
Cause No.: 74 L 866 Circuit Court St. Clair County
Summary: Date of Accident: 11/12/1973. Wrongful death action. 12:55 PM at Tamarack Country Club, O'Fallon, IL. Deceased struck and killed by truck driven by Co-Defendant as deceased crossing roadway on country club.

MOSBOCHER, ELROY, for the use and benefit of Economy Fire and Casualty Company v GENERAL MOTORS CORPORATION
Amount of Suit: $4,200.00
Attorney: Norman Kinder
File No.: R653A-22137 - Temple
Cause No.: 73 LM 1552 Circuit Court St. Clair County
Summary: Date of Accident: 4/26/1971. Suit on express new car warranty. Plaintiff purchased 1971 Chevrolet Caprice on 3/5/71. Automobile destroyed by fire on 4/26/71

LEAVY, ROBERT v GM&O RR Co.
Amount of Suit: $275,000.00
Attorney: Walker and Williams (Stutsman)
File No.: PI-37774 - Johnston
Cause No.: 72-L-290 Circuit Court Madision County
Summary: Date of Accident: 2/19/1972. Defendant's yards at Venice, IL. Plaintiff, an employee of Leuking Transfer Co., injured while loading trailers on railroad cars.

STEVENSON, MARIE v GENERAL MOTORS, et al (Royal Globe)
Amount of Suit: $50,000.00
Attorney: Dixon and McDonnell
File No.:   R653A-26943 - Langhammer
Cause No.:   72-2687 Circuit Court St. Clair County
Summary: Date of Accident: 6/3/1972. St. Clair at 18th Street, East St. Louis. Plaintiff, a passenger in a 1970 Cadillac ambulance owned by Pete Gaerdner, was thrown from the ambulance when it collided with automobiles being driven by Co-Defendants.

WUERZ, MAYBELL v EAST ST. LOUIS AND INTERURBAN WATER COMPANY, et al (Royal Globe)
Amount of Suit: $40,000.00
Attorney: Baltz, Guyman, Jennings and Tedesco
File No.:   R653A-23077 - Temple
Cause No.:   72-2605 Circuit Court St. Clair County
Summary: Date of Accident: 12/6/1971. 9:00 AM on sidewalk on State Street at 85th Street. Plaintiff, a pedestrain, fell into hole when earth gave way under her.

BRICKER, ELIZABETH M., a minor v BI-STATE TRANSIT SYSTEM, et al (Transit Cas)
Amount of Suit: $3,500.00
Attorney: C.E. Heiligenstein
File No.:   10-11-10166-001 - L.F. Stephens
Cause No.:   72-2367 Circuit Court St. Clair County
Summary: Date of Accident: 9/7/1972. 2200 N. Illinois Street, Belleville. Plaintiff, leaving Bi-State bus, crossed in front of bus and was struck by Co-Defendant.

REED, PHILIP, a minor, v PARLANTE, DR. VINCENT J.
(Commercial Union - other case: Kimbro v)
Amount of Suit: $500,000.00
Attorney: James Buchmiller
File No.: McWilliams
Cause No.: 73-L-15 Circuit Court Montgomery County
Summary: Date of Accident: 2/9/1972. Malpractice case. Defendant saw 5 month old Plaintiff and diagnosed condition as acute pharyngitis. Plaintiff apparently suffered from meningitis and is now mentally defective and blind.

FOUST, TERRY v GENERAL MOTORS CORPORATION, et al
(Royal Globe)
Amount of Suit: $25,000.00
Attorney: Sprague, Sprague and Ysursa
File No.: R645A-26992 - English
Cause No.: 72-2241 Circuit Court St. Clair County
Summary: Date of Accident: 6/11/1971. Route 50 and Frey Lane, St. Clair County, IL. Plaintiff, traveling east on Route 50, struck by Co-Defendant's 65 Pontiac. Plaintiff claims brakes on Pontiac were defective because of flexible brake hoses.

MERCURIO, LUCILLE, et al v BURPO, CARL E., et al (Hartford)
Amount of Suit: $150,000.00
Attorney: Chapman, Strawn, Kinder, Talbert and Chapman
File No.: Greer
Cause No.: 7003775 Circuit Court St. Clair County
Summary: Date of Accident: 1/25/1967. Malpractice case. Plaintiff operated on by Drs. Miller and Baldree. Thereafter, became patient of Defendant. Plaintiff claims Defendant failed to properly diagnose Plaintiff's condition.

WAYNE COUNTY BANK, et al v JACK H. PURCELL, et a.
Amount of Suit: $210,210.81
Attorney: Craig and Craig
Co-Defendants: Paul Riggle, Flora, IL;
John Carlon, Ft. Lauderdale, FL;
Robert Lucke, Annapolis, MD
Summary: Four banks suing for amount due on notes

ENGELMANN, FRED v NORFOLK AND WESTERN RAILWAY COMPANY & WAYNE JONES
Amount of Suit: $200,000.00
Attorney: Paul Pratt
File No.: 161-4448 - Sample
Cause No.: 72-L-83 Circuti Court Madison County
Summary: Date of Accident: 7/29/1970. 11:40 AM at unloading pit of Illinois Valley Asphalt Co., north of Pittsfield, IL. Plaintiff, an employee of Illinois Valley, was unloading gravel car when Defendant connected on to cut of cars and started pulling same forcing Plaintiff to drop into gravel pit below car.

SIEVERS, DANIEL, a minor, etc. v GENERAL MOTORS, et al
(Royal Globe)
Amount of Suit: $100,000.00
Attorney: Pratt and Mosley
File No.: R653A-23484 - Heim
Cause No.: 72-L-60 Circuit Court Madison County
Summary: Date of Accident: 2/8/1971. Hardin-Brussels Road near Geers, Hill Road, 9 1/2 miles south of Hardin, IL. Co-Defendant Mossman, driving school bus south on Hardin-Brussels Road, stopped at intersection of Geers Hill Road to let mentally retarded Plaintiff off of bus. Plaintiff started crossing Hardin-Brussels from west to east and was struck by southbound Co-Defendant, Canepa, driving 1965 Chevrolet Impala. Plaintiff claims rearview mirror on Chevrolet obstructed Canepa's vision.

HAINES, PAUL R. v FULLER BROS. MASONRY CONSTRUCTION CO.
(Underwriters)
Amount of Suit: $13,000.00
Attorney: Listeman, Bandy and Hamilton
File No.: 46 GL 81658 - Gerding
Cause No.: 71-929 Circuit Court St. Clair County
Summary: Date of Accident: 12/3/1970. Scaffold Act case. 3:30 PM. Plaintiff, employed by Western Architectural Iron Co., on job for Central Illinois Public Service Co. at Coffeen, IL. Plaintiff riding a man lift when struck by concrete block.

CROWDER, DARYL, a minor, et al v WIESE CUSHMAN, INC., et al
(Maryland Casual Co.)
Amount of Suit: $70,000.00
Attorney: Walker and Williams (Imber)
File No.: 560-A-112947 Schmittling
Cause No.: Civ 70-4205 St. Clair County
Summary: Date of Accident: 7/2/1970. 5:30 PM on Illnois State Rt. 3 near Jean's Tavern in Dupo, IL. Defendant south on Rt. 3 came upon Co-Defendant stopped to make left turn. Defendant slid centerline and collided head on with Plaintiffs northbound automobile.

WEISE, ROY v GENERAL MOTORS CORPORATION, et al
(Royal Globe)
Amount of Suit: $35,000.00
Attorney: C.E. Heiligenstein
File No.: Heim R653A-23376
Cause No.: 71-3082 Circuit Court St. Clair County
Summary: Date of Accident: 5/9/1970. Intersection of Rts. 4 & 138 in Macoupin County, IL. Plaintiff driving 1968 Chevrolet truck north on Rt. 4 collided with Co-Defendant traveling east on Rt. 138. Plaintiff claims his injuries were made more severe because of front axle spring or securing mechanism of the truck breaking and coming apart.

REPPY, BEATRICE, et al v USSELMANN, GREGORY, et al (Underwriters)
Amount of Suit: Count I, $15,000.00; Count II, $50,000.00
Attorney: Goldenhersh and Goldenhersh (David)
File No.: 46 AP 81600 - Gerding
Cause No.: 72-13-USDC E. St. Louis
Summary: Date of Accident: 11/9/1970. Count I for personal Injuries; Count II for wrongful death. 7:45 PM on Rt. 3 in Red Bud, IL. Plaintiff's north on Rt. 3 when Co-Defendant entered Rt. 3 from west on Shiloh Dr. and turned north in front of Plaintiff. Plaintiff swerved to left and onto wrong side of street and collided with southbound Defendant head on.

CARTER, SHERRY LYNN, a minor v. DOCTER, MARVIN P.
(Hartford) (See also McKittrick v. Docter)
Amount of Suit: $75,000.00
Attorney: Meyer and Meyer
File No.: 46 KAL 34140 Yoakam
Cause No.: 70-L-346 Circuit Court Madison County
Summary: Date of Accident: 1/4/1970. 3:45 PM. North Keebler Rd. at Cathy Ct., Collinsville, IL. Defendant south on Keebler. Plaintiff east on Cathy Ct. made right turn onto Keebler in front of Defendant. Plaintiff arrested for failure to yield right of way.

BARTON, EZEKIAL v. TERMINAL RAILROAD v. GENERAL MOTORS
(Royal Globe)
Amount of Suit: $200,000.00
Attorney: Talbert and Plaintiff Terminal - Richard Boyle
File No.: R653A-23443 Heim
Cause No.: 70-I-704 Circuit Court Madison County
Summary: Date of Accident: 11/3/1968. FELA and Boiler Inspection Act case v Terminal RR. Terminal seeks indemnity from GM. Madison Yards of Terminal RR. Plaintiff claims he was injured on locomotive unit #1240.

CARROLL, CHRISTINE v SIOUX CITY AND NEW ORLEANS BARGE LINES, INC., a corporation
(See Robert Carroll v. Sioux City - Circuit Court Madison City)
Amount of Suit: $9,900.00
Attorney: Frank Conner
File No.: 46 GL 79801 Gerding
Cause No.: 71-307 Circuit Court St. Clair County
Summary: Date of Accident: 2/7/1969. Wife's loss of consortium case. Jones Act case. 4:30 PM. Motor vessel "Mr. Cole" in Alton, IL. Plaintiff's husband was injured as he was unloading rubber pads from a pickup truck

CARROLL, ROBERT v. SIOUX CITY AND NEW ORLEANS BARGE LINES, INC., (Underwriters)
(See Christine Carroll v. Sioux City - Circuit Court St. Clair County)
Amount of Suit: $900,000.00
Attorney: Wagner, Conner, Ferguson, Bertrand and Baker
File No.: MC 69-1755 Fraley
Cause No.: 70-L-841 Circuit Court Madison County
Summary: Date of Accident: 2/7/1969. Jones Act case. 4:30 PM. Motor vessel "Mr. Cole" in Alton, IL. Plaintiff was injured as he was unloading rubber pads from a pickup truck.

DOOLIN, LEO E. v NORFOLK & WESTERN RAILWAY CO.
Amount of Suit: $300,000.00
Attorney: Freeark, Gunn and Harvey
File No.: 161-4528, L-12587 Sample
Cause No.: 72-L-538 Circuit Court Madison County
Summary: Date of Accident: 10/3/1969. FELA case. 8:20 AM at Taylorville, IL. Plaintiff, an engineer deadheading on freight train DS-11 to Taylorville, attempted to get off of diesel as train was traveling about 10 miles per hour. Plaintiff slipped and fell and fractured tibia of left leg. At present he has lost $42,951.78 in lost wages. Plaintiffs attorney demanded $150,000.00

CANADY, JESSIE L., Admr. V. GENERAL MOTORS, et al
(See Roberts v. General Motors)
Amount of Suit: $100,000.00
Attorney: Listeman, Bandy and Hamilton
File No.: R653A-22993 Heim
Cause No.: 72-2227 Circuit Court St. Clair County
Summary: Date of Accident: 6/11/1971. 1:30 PM. Ten people, including deceased and Plaintiff were riding in a 1965 Pontiac stationwagon traveling west on Park Blvd. in Chester, IL. Brakes failed, car ran into Mississippi. Seven dead - three injured.

ROBERTS, DARWIN B., Admr., etc. v GENERAl MOTORS
(Royal-Globe) (See Canady v. General Motors)
Amount of Suit: $100,000.00
Attorney: Listeman, Bandy and Hamiilton
File No.: R653A-22993 Heim
Cause No.: 71-2928 Circuit Court St. Clair County
Summary: Date of Accident: 6/11/1971. 1:30 PM. Ten people, including deceased and Plaintiff were riding in a 1965 Pontiac stationwagon traveling west on Park Blvd. in Chester, IL. Brakes failed, car ran into Mississippi. Seven dead - three injured.

CLARK, CHARLES, Admr., etc. v. GENERAL MOTORS CORP., et al (See also Roberts v. General Motors; Canaday v. General Motors)
Amount of Suit: Four wrongful deaths at $100,000.00
Attorney: Brady, Donovan and Hatch;
Co-Defendant - Leskera
File No.: R653A-22993 Temple
Cause No.: 73-L-001042 St. Clair County
Summary: Date of Accident: 6/11/1971. Wrongful death action for four children. 1:30 PM, four children riding in 1965 Pontiac stationwagon driven by their mother traveling west on Park Blvd. in Chester, IL. Brakes failed, car ran into Mississippi.

GILBERT, JANICE C., et al v McDANIEL, WILLIAM, et al
(Hartford)
Amount of Suit: IV, $30,000; V, $7,500.00; VI, $4,000.00
Attorney: Bock and Stenger
File No.: 46 KAL 37285 Greer
Cause No.: CIV 70 4159 Circuit Court St. Clair County
Summary: Date of Accident: 6/13/1970. 11:00 PM, St. Clair Avenue near 42nd St. in E. St. Louis. Plaintiffs were driving and riding in Defendant's automobile and traveling east on St. Clair. To avoid another automobile, Plaintiff Gilbert applied brakes. Plaintiffs claim defective brakes caused car to overturn.

ASHMANN, DAVID v N & W RAILWAY Co.
Amount of Suit: $150,000.00
Attorney: Haley, Frederickson & Stubbs
File No.: Lawsuit 161-4317 Sample
Cause No.: 71-2074 Circuit Court Belleville
Summary: Date of Accident: 8/12/1968. FELA case. 2:30 PM Middle Yrad, Brooklyn, IL. Plaintiff was inspecting locomotive to be returned to service when his foot slipped from a step causing him to land hard on his feet. Plaintiff demanded $5,000.00. Defendant offered $2,500.00. Plaintiff's attorney now demands $50,000.00

McKITTRICK, KARLA, a minor v OCTER, MARVIN P.
(Hartford) (See also Carter v. Docter)
Amount of Suit: $25,000.00
Attorney: Meyer and Meyer
File No.: 46 KAL 34140 Yoakam
Cause No.: 70-L-496 Circuit Court Madison County
Set for Trial: <
Summary: Date of Accident: 1/4/1970. 3:45 PM. North Keebler Rd. at Cathy Ct., Collinsville, IL. Defendant south on Keebler. Plaintiff east on Cathy Ct. made right turn onto Keebler in front of Defendant. Plaintiff arrested for failure to yield right of way.

CARLTON, ROBERT S. v GENERAL MOTORS & TERMINAL RAILROAD
(Royal-Globe)
Amount of Suit: $150,000.00
Attorney: McGlynn and McGlynn
File No.:   R653A-14825 Roach, J.S.
Cause No.:   70-3356 Circuit Court St. Clair County
Summary: Date of Accident: 5/27/1968. 8:00 PM, General Motors Plant, St. Louis, MO. Plaintiff, a switchman for Terminal, injured back when throwing derail at Fisher Body track No. 1.

KECK, CHARLES v NORFOLK AND WESTERN RAILWAY CO.
Amount of Suit: $75,000.00
Attorney: Chapman, Talbert and Chapman
File No.:   L-12165 Sample
Cause No.:   71-L-211 Circuit Court Madison County
Summary: Date of Accident: 1/23/1971. FELA case. 8:00 PM, at Luther Yards, St. Louis, MO. Plaintiff, a carman, attempting to board caboose injured his left knee. Medial meniscus removed.

ILLINOIS STATE TRUST COMPANY v TEAGLE, ERNEST, et al
(Employers-Commercial Union)
Amount of Suit: $100,000.00
Attorney: John E. Norton
File No.:   K4-3336 McWilliams
Cause No.:   72-1325 Circuit Court St. Clair County
Summary: Malpractice case. Wrongful death. Defendant operated on decedent three times. Decedent died 5/21/70.

HAHN, FRANK v NORFOLK AND WESTERN RAILWAY CO.
(Two Suits)
Amount of Suit: $15,000.00
Attorney: Chapman, Talbert and Chapman
File No.: Sample
Cause No.: 72-M-240 Circuit Court Madison County
Summary: Date of Accident: 11/23/1971. 11:45 AM at Madison repair track, Madison, IL. Plaintiff claims injured knees after being in kneeling position.

REYNOLDS, GRADY v UNION ELECTRIC COMPANY, et al
(Royal Globe)
Amount of Suit: $2,000.00
Attorney: Cohn, Korein, Kunin and Brennan (Lakin)
File No.: R653A 23317 Heim
Cause No.: Civ 72-1583 Circuit Court St. Clair County
Summary: Date of Accident: 12/17/1971. 10:00 AM at Walnut and 4th St., St. Louis, MO. Plaintiff, west on Walnut and stopped at stoplight, rear ended by Defendant. Defendant settled and obtained release from Plaintiff.

RYAN, NICHOLAS v NORFOLK AND WESTERN RAILWAY CO.
Amount of Suit: $50,000.00
Attorney: Chapman, Strawn, Kinder and Talbert
File No.: L-11901 Sample
Cause No.: 70-L-352 Circuit Court Madison County
Summary: Date of Accident: 2/20/1970. 8:15 AM, No. 4 track TOFC ramp, Madison, IL. Plaintiff received electric shock using electric wrench loading piggyback trailers.

CLEMENTS, MELVIN v G.H. STERNBERG AND COMPANY
(Harford)
Amount of Suit: $100,000.00
Attorney: Wm. Schooley
File No.:   Yoakam
Cause No.:   70-L-125 Circuit Court Madison County
Summary: Date of Accident: 3/28/1969. U.S. Army Depot, Gr. City, IL. Defendant was general contractor to do work for U.S. government at Army Depot. Defendant subcontracted with Plaintiff's employer, George Slay Co., to perform brick work. Plaintiff was hod carrier and was injured when a rung from a ladder broke causing Plaintiff to fall.

HOLLIDAY, BURNELL H. v FIX, MARLIN E., et al v GENERAL MOTORS
(Royal Globe)
Amount of Suit: $50,000.00
Attorney: Sprague, Sprague and Ysursa
                    3rd Party P - Wagner, Conner, et al (Bauman)
File No.:   R 653a-21696 English
Cause No.:   71-137 Circuit Court St. Clair County
Summary: Date of Accident: 12/20/1970. St. Clair County at Rt. 50 and 94th St. Plaintiff traveling west on Rt. 50 rear ended by Defendant. Defendant seeks common law indemnity against manufacturer of truck.

SPRADLIN, LINDA v TERMINAL RAILROAD ASSOCIATION, et al
(Plaintiff Case)
Summary: Date of Accident: 2/14/1970. 4:00 AM. 19th St. and railroad tracks. Plaintiff west on 19th St., stopped suddenly for northbound Terminal engine crossing street. The tower did not lower gate or turn on flashing lights until after engine was in street. When Plaintiff stopped suddenly, she was rear ended by uninsured motorist.

SCHAEFER, LARRY v NORFOLK AND WESTERN RAILWAY CO.
Amount of Suit: $200,000.00
Attorney: James T. Williamson
File No.:   161-4388 Sample
Cause No.:   71-L-552 Circuit Court Madison County
Summary: Date of Accident: 5/3/1971. 9:00 AM, Brooklyn Yards, Brooklyn, IL. Plaintiff, a crane operator, strained his back attempting to lift a switchpoint which had caught a fellow employee's hand.

BAKER, LANCE v NORFOLK AND WESTERN RAILWAY CO.
Amount of Suit: $200,000.00
Attorney: Edward Stubbs, Jr.
File No.:   161-4595 (L-12645) Sample
Cause No.:   73-L-000881 Circuit Court St. Clair County
Summary: Date of Accident: 2/3/1971. 9:30 PM in Brooklyn Yards, Brooklyn, IL. Plaintiff, a switchman, was riding on side step of switch engine and when it coupled into piggyback car bridge ramp fell forward striking Plaintiff's left arm.

McCOY, LINDA v CHEROKEE PRODUCTS CO., et al
(Royal Globe)
Amount of Suit: $200,000.00
Attorney: Rex Carr
File No.:   Royal Globe, Wisdom
Cause No.:   74-L-1750 Circuit Court St. Clair County
Summary: Date of Accident: 9/9/1973. Calvin Johnson Nursing Home. Plaintiff, an employee of nursing home, caught her left hand in elevator manufactured by Defendant.

ARCHITECTURAL DESIGN v COMMERCIAL UNION
Amount of Suit: $30,000.00
Attorney: Donald L. Smith
Cause No.: 75-L-2031 Circuit Court St. Clair County
Summary: Garnishment Action

ROTH, HARRY W. v. ALTON & SOUTHERN RAILWAY CO. et al, Paragon Division of Portec, Inc., third party Plaintiff v GENERAL MOTORS CORPORATION, third party Defendant
Attorney: Callis and Hartman;Paragon - Hoagland Maucker
Ill Term. - Gundlach, etc.;
AO Smith - Dunham, Moman, etc.;
Alton & Southern - Walker & Williams
Cause No.: 76-L-454 Circuit Court Madison County
Summary: Date of Accident: 4/20/1976. Safety Appliance Act and FELA Case. Plaintiff, switchman for Alton & Southern, injured at Gateway Yard of Alton & Southern while working on a TTX car. Injury due to defective "ear latch" on a "spacer container." The spacer container manufactured by Moore Iron Works.

SMITH, MARGARET-JEAN, Admr. V. GENERAL MOTORS
(Royal Globe)
Amount of Suit: $500,000.00
Attorney: David M. Duree, Kenney, Leritz & Reinert
Cause No.: 77-L-929 Circuit Court Madison County
Summary: Date of Accident: 12/17/1976. Products liability case for wrongful death of Wm. N. Smith. Smith, operating 1970 or 1972 Cadillac near Princeton in Bureau County, IL. Auto left highway and struck something. Suit filed alleging that the Cadillac was not equipped with an energy absorbing steering column or that the energy absorbing steering column did not work. Suit is brought under the Illinois Wrongful Death Statute.

WOOLARD, J.P. v. U.S. STEEL v PEABODY COAL Co.
(Old Republic)
Amount of Suit: Excess of $15,000.
Attorney: P - Carl Runge; U.S. Steel - Larry Hepler;
P&S Grain - Bill Hoagland
File No.: 906267
Cause No.: 79-L-1067 Circuit Court Madison County
Summary: Date of Accident: 11/8/1977. Will Scarlet Mine at Stone Fort, IL. Plaintiff, an employee of Peabody, claims he sustained carcinoma of the larynx when exposed to an excesssive amount of ammonia which was manufactured by U.S. Steel and distributed by U.S. Grain. Plaintiff sues U.S. Steel on strict liability. U.S. Steel seeks contribution from Peabody.

BRUCKERHOFF, N.H. v LOUIS H. SEXAUER, et al
(Dearing, Richeson, Roberts & Wegmann)
Amount of Suit: $250,000.00
Attorney: Wagner, Bertrand, Bauman & Schmieder
Cause No.: Removed from Circuit Court St. Clair County to USDC, East District
Summary: Plaintiff cliams that Defendants unlawfully converted timber from real estate to their own use.

HARRIS, GLOVER v TERMINAL RAILROAD v. GENERAL MOTORS CORPORATION (Royal-Globe)
Amount of Suit: $50,000.00
Attorney: P - Chapman & Chapman;
3P - Roberts Gunclach and Lee
File No.: GM File MS-04519
Cause No.: 75-L-256 Circuit Court Madison County
Summary: Date of Accident: 2/25/1975. FELA case against railroad which brings indemnity action against Genral Motors Corp.

RUSICK, RICHARD v GENERAL MOTORS CORPORATION, et al
(Royal-Globe)
Amount of Suit: $750,000.00
Attorney: Chapman & Chapman (Peel)
File No.: Wisdom - June Morgan
Cause No.: 75-L-277 Circuit Court Madison County
Summary: Date of Accident: 3/7/1975. Products case involving 1974 Chevy pickup truck. Plaintiff operating truck on Old IL Rt. 40 near Lantern's crossing in Madision County, IL.

ANDERSON, LEONARD HUGH v GATEWAY HARBOR SERVICVE, INC.
(Joe Kortenhof)
Amount of Suit: $75,000.00
Attorney: Cohn, Korein, Kunin & Brennan
File No.: EM-01756
Cause No.: 72-1435 Circuit Court St. Clair County
Summary: Date of Accident: 7/17/1970. Maritime & Jones Act case. Plaintiff, a deckhand on M/V/ Erna-A, injured while engaged in his duties.

KLEINIGGER, RONALD J. v J.I. CASE CO, PETERSON TWOHIG and DUE, INC. and FLUOR BROTHERS CONSTRUCTION CO.
(Commercial Union - Bloomington)
Amount of Suit: $10,000.00
Attorney: Bill Schooley
File No.: Bob Tuma
Cause No.: 77-LM-314
Summary: Date of Accident: 3/11/1977. Structural Work Act case. Plaintiff injured while working at J.I. Case Co. in Bloomington, IL.

RAINWATERS, HILMON v NEW YORK CENTRAL RAILROAD CO.
Amount of Suit: $75,000.00
Attorney: Rex Carr
File No.: 7.23704 - Olson
Cause No.: 63-221 Circuit Court St. Clair County
Set for Trial: 11/30/1961
Summary: Date of Accident: 2/24/1961. FELA case. 2:15 AM - lower pass track, Brooklyn Yards, E. St. Louis, IL. Plaintiff, a car inspector, claims he hurt back while closing door of boxcar No. DT and I 4007.

PASTROVICk, JOS. v MASCOUTAH GRAIN
(Commercial Union)
Amount of Suit: $100,000.00
Attorney: Sprague
File No.: Employers K4-6749
Cause No.: Bill 73-2534
Summary: Date of Accident: 5/16/1973. Leased liquid fertilizer spreader from Defendant. Tractor had no guard over power latch off spline. Planitiff got off tractor and got entangled with universal.

GAUGES, ROBERT STEVE v INTERNATIONAL HARVESTER CO.
(Royal-Globe)
Amount of Suit: $1,500,000.00
Attorney: Bruce Cook
File No.: 5S653A-43550 Wisdom
Cause No.: 76-L-2050 Circuit Court St. Clair County
Summary: Date of Accident: 4/19/1974. Product Liability Case. McEvers Farm, Green County, IL. Plaintiff operating IH Farmall 756 tractor when it burst into flames seriously burning Plaintiff.

GARREN, ARNOLD v INTERNATIONAL HARVESTER CO. et al
Attorney: Hanagan & Dousman
File No.: 653A-46294 English-Croft
Cause No.: 77-L-2383 Circuit Court St. Clair County
Summary: Date of Accident: 10/28/1976. Product Liability involving 1975 International Harvester 1600 2-ton truck. Brake failure, 3 PM at Richview, IL. Plaintiff unloading truck when Harvester truck collided witn truck Plaintiff unloading.

REBER, ALAN J. v GOODAL RUBBER COMPANY et al
 (Royal-Globe)
Amount of Suit: Actual Damages - $500,000.00
 Punitive Damages - $1,000,000.00
Attorney: John E. Norton
File No.: 5R653A-35135 - Wisdom
Cause No.: 73-L-2473 Circuit Court St. Clair County
Summary: Date of Accident: 9/25/1972. 8:00 PM - Columbiana Seed Co, Wolf Lake, IL. Planitiff delivering propane gas which ignited and burned Plaintiff.

WRIGHT, KATHY, a minor, etc. v GENERAL MOTORS (Royal-Globe)
Amount of Suit: $82,000.00
Attorney: Jack Norton
File No.: Temple
Cause No.: 74-I-001735 Circuit Court St. Clair County

RYE, STEVEN v INTERNATIONAL HARVESTER, et al
(Royal-Globe)
Amount of Suit: $300,000.00
Attorney: Wiseman, Shaikewitz and McGivern
File No.:   S653A-25987 Temple
Cause No.:   72-L-29 Circuit Court Madison County
Summary: Date of Accident: 9/10/1972. Products liability case. 11:00 Am Route 67, St. Charles County, MO. Plaintiff, driving Internatinal Harvestor Metro-Mite Van truck collided with something, throwing Plaintiff from truck. Plaintiff claims truck should have been equipped with seat belt.

NISCHWITZ, MARK v OBEAR NESTER GLASS CO.
(Commercial Union)
Amount of Suit: $50,000.00
Attorney: Reed, Armstrong, Gorman & Coffey (Peel)
File No.:   Wilde
Cause No.:   73-L-529 Circuit Court Madison County
Summary: Date of Accident: 1/13/1973. Scaffolding Act case

HUNTER, ELIZABETH v STACKABLE, DR. WILLIAM R., et al (Commercial Union)
Amount of Suit: $500,000.00
Attorney: Meyer and Kaucher
File No.:   Wilde
Cause No.:   73-L-48 Circuit Court Jefferson County
Summary: Date of Accident: 6/14/1972. Malpractice case. Plaintiff injured in auto accident and hospitalized at Good Samaritan Hospital and claims injuries aggravated by treatment received from Defendant.

MILON, NICOLE v. VILLAGE OF ALORTON and THOMAS WINDOM
(Royal-Globe)
Amount of Suit: $7,500.00
Attorney: David Goldenhersh
File No.:   Wisdom
Cause No.:   74-LM-2811 Circuit Court St. Clair County
Summary: Date of Accident: 11/9/1973. 1:20 PM Bond Avenue near 50th Street, Centerville, IL. Plaintiff westbound on Bond Avenue rear ended by Defendant.

MAGERS, MICHAEL v. GENERAL MOTORS COMPANY, et al
(Royal-Globe)
Amount of Suit: $3,400.00
Attorney: Thomas LeChien
File No.:   R653A-24441 Klauke
Cause No.:   71-1812 Circuit Court St. Clair County
Summary: Date of Accident: 4/8/1972. 900 block of Camp Jackson Road (Rte. 157) near the Mo-Pac tracks in Cahokia, IL. Plaintiff's 1972 Chevrolet Malibu stopped and was struck by Co-Defendant. Plaintiff claims automobile was defective and this is what caused it to stop.

CONDON, JOHN L., et al v GINN, MAX, d/b/a Ginn Trucking Service
Amount of Suit: Count I - $400,00.00; Count II - $100,000.00
Attorney: Melvin D. Benitz
File No.:   Temple
Cause No.:   CV 74-1D U.S. District Court, Danville
Summary: Date of Accident: 1/31/1972. 1:30 AM Interstate 70 - 7.5 miles west of Efffingham. Defendant traveling west rear ended by Plaintiffs.

SHELBY, JAMES & MARY v. KROGER COMPANY, et al v. H. B. KENNERLY & SON (Royal-Globe)
Amount of Suit: $100,00.00
Attorney: P - McGlynn & McGlynn;
                   Dunham, Boman, Leskera & Churchill (Francis)
File No.:   X0653826939-00 Temple
Cause No.:   72-1988 Circuit Court St. Clair County
Summary: Date of Accident: 1/6 or 1/7/1972. Plaintiff's claim they contracted hepatitis from eating oysters which they purchased at Kroger in Chaokia, IL. Kroger seeks indemnity from Kennerly who sold oysters to Kroger.

BURNLEY, LARRy D., ADMR. V BURPO, CARL E., et al
(Employers-Commercial Union)
Amount of Suit: $750,000.00
Attorney: Callis and Filcoff
File No.:   Kf-4846 McWilliams
Cause No.:   Circuit Court City Madison County
Summary: Date of Accident: 12/13/1971. Wrongful death action based on medical malpractice. Defendant inserted IUD in deceased. Deceased died 12/19/71 as a result of ruptered uterus.

SUMNER, RICHARD A., et al v WILLIAMS, HERSCHEL W.
(Commercial Union)
Amount of Suit: $65,000.00
Attorney: Trotier and Brian
File No.:   K4-760676 - Wilde
Cause No.:   74-CIV-420 Circuit Court Randolph County
Summary: Date of Accident: 8/9/1974. 3:45 PM Route 155, 1 mile south of Ruma, IL. Plaintiff in automobile traveling south on Rt. 155 collided with Defendant entering from side road.

BELLEVILLE NATIONAL SAVINGS BANK Admr., Estate of Joel R. Bonifield, deceased and v KEITH BONIFIELD v GEO. E. HILGARD POST No. 58, Americn Legion (Commercial Union)
Amount of Suit: $98,572.86
Attorney: John E. Norton
File No.: K4-7019 Wilde
Cause No.: 73-L-2707 Circuit Court St. Clair County
Summary: Date of Accident: 7/4/1973. Death case. 1:30 AM American Legion Freedom Farm near Freeburg, IL. Deceased, who had not paid, dove from diving board at swimming lake at 1:30 AM and struck bottom. Received injuries restuling in his death.

MOUSHMOF, MILCO v DELAND FARMERS, et al v THE MEL JARVIS CONST. CO., INC. (Employers-Commercial Union)
Amount of Suit: $100,000.00
Attorney: P - Ryan and Heller;
Deland - Wagner, Conner (Bauman)
File No.: W2 OBI-Cassin
Cause No.: 72-L-182 Circuit Court Madison County
Summary: Date of Accident: 7/2/1971. Wrongful death action. 11:00 AM at Deland Farmers, Deland, IL. Plaintiff, an employee of Jarvis electrocuted while operating cement mixer. Deland Farmer's sues Jarvis for indemnity.

SMITH, GEORGE v DELANO, Jay
(Northwestern National Insurance Group)
Amount of Suit: $50,000.00
Attorney: Wiseman, Shaikewitz and McGivern
File No.: 82-2423 - Gates
Cause No.: 74-L-783 Circuit Court Madison County
Summary: Date of Accident: 2/19/1974. 11:30 AM - Defendant's premises at 530 Henry St., Alton, IL. Plaintiff fell down steps and claims hearing loss. Plaintiff demanded $215, Plaintiff's attorney demanded $15,000.00

BRITTON, FRANCES JANE v O. BALLESTEROS and A.H. ROBINS COMPANY
(Commercial Union)
Amount of Suit: $50,000.00
Attorney: Callis and Filcoff
File No.: Wilde
Cause No.: 74-L-585 Circuit Court Madison County
Summary: Date of Accident: 11/7/1972. Malpractice case. Defendant inserted "Kaldon Shield" IUD NP. Plaintiff claims it perforated uterus. IUD subsequently surgically removed by antoher doctor.

DETERMAN, NORMAN, et al v GENERAL MOTORS CORP., et al
Amount of Suit: $15,500.00
Attorney: Norton and Strange
File No.: Robert Culver (GM)
Cause No.: 75-3016 USDC E. St. Louis
Summary: Breach of warranty of fitness of action involving a 23 foot Open Road Motor Home purchased by Plaintiff's on 6/7/74.

MORROW, BEN v UNION FIDELITY LIFE INSURANCE CO.
(Union Fidelity)
Amount of Suit: $986.85
Attorney: William Wimmer
File No.:   Pol: 1-5328368 - Karyn Feeney
Cause No.:   SC 75-1947
Summary: Suit on health insurance policy.

HAROIAN, VAHRAM v NORFOLK AND WESTERN RR CO.
Amount of Suit: $250,000.00
Attorney: Frederickson, Stubbs and Abele
File No.:   161-4611, L-12673 Sample
Cause No.:   73-L-1130 St. Clair County
Summary: Date of Accident: 5/6/1972. FELA case. 1:30 PM at Luther Yards. Plaintiff attempting to throw switch #40 injured neck resulting in cervical disc operation.

MEISTER, PAULINE v ST. CLAIR SQUARE, INC. a corporation and MAY STORES SHOPPING CENTERS, INC., a corporation (Underwriters)
Amount of Suit: $75,000.00
Attorney: Harry J. Sterling
File No.:   046-2F5008 - Gerding
Cause No.:   76-L-1621 Circuit Court St. Clair County
Summary: Date of Accident: 12/26/1974. St. Clair Square Mall. Plaintiff slipped and fell near water fountain. Plaintiff's attorney demanded $20,000. Defendant hopes to settle for $12,000.00

MURPHY, GERALD v CLARK OIL & REFINING CORPORATION v G. HELMKAMP EXCAVATING & TRUCKING CO.
(Royal-Globe) (See Perrin)
Amount of Suit: $150,000.00
Attorney: Pratt & Kardis
File No.: R653A-26758 - Wisdom
Cause No.: 74-L-610 Circuit Court Madison County
Set for Trial: 11/18/1974
Summary: Date of Accident: 11/29/1972. Premises of Clark Oil in Hartford, IL. Clark Oil had contract with G. Helmkamp Excavating to remove sludge from tank. Plaintiff, an employee of Helmkamp, hurt his back. Count I violation of Structural Work Act; Count II failure to provide a reasonably safe place to work.

ECKMAN, THOMAS D. v LOUISIANA TOWING CO., INC.
(Kortenhof)
Amount of Suit: $100,000.00
Attorney: Cohn, Carr, Korein, Kunin and Brennan
File No.: Kortenhof
Cause No.: 74-L-977 Circuit Court St. Clair County
Summary: Date of Accident: 1/9/1974. Jones Act and Maritime case. On MV Cayuga on Illinois River near Meradosia, IL. Plaintiff, a seaman, slipped on one of the barges.

STAMBAUGH, MELVIN C. v INTERNATIONAL HARVESTER COMPANY
(Royal-Globe)
Amount of Suit: $200,000.00
Attorney: Bruce Cook
File No.: D-2048 - Bill Pell - Wisdom - 2S653A-45225
Cause No.: 76-L-2775 Circuit Court St. Clair County
Summary: Date of Accident: 5/17/1975. Products Liability case involving International Harvester Farm Tractor Model F-706, Serial No. 2393. Plaintiff claims as he was operating tractor, it exploded and injured him.

CUNNINGHAM, JUDITH L. v EAST ST. LOUIS & INTERURBAN WATER COMPANY, et al (Royal-Globe)
Amount of Suit: $100,000.00
Attorney: Wm. Brandt
File No.: R653A-26757 - Wisdom
Cause No.: 73-L-233 Circuit Court Madison County
Summary: Date of Accident: 11/28/1972. 25th & Grand Ave., Granite City. Defendant installing new fire hydrant. Plaintiff slipped and fell while attempting to cross intersection.

McMULLIN, ROBERT v YAMAHA et al
Amount of Suit: $1,500,000.00
Attorney: Miller-Leskera; Yamaha - Gagan; Zwick - John Bauman
Cause No.: 71-1007 Circuit Court St. Clair County
Summary: Plaintiff Case

ENNES, JOHN A. et al v MID-AMERICA COACHES, INC., et al (Joe Kortenhof)
Amount of Suit: $75,000.00
Attorney: Rarick and Cadigan
File No.: Joe Kortenhof
Cause No.: US District Court, Southern District
Summary: Date of Accident: 3/31/1973. Colorado State Highway 24, 4 miles east of Genoa, Colorado. Plaintiff, a passenger on Defendant's westbound bus which collided with co-dfenedant's eastbound tractor-trailer.

SCOTT, THOMAS E. v GENERAL MOTORS CORPORATION
(Royal-Globe)
Amount of Suit: $2,000.00
Attorney: Wham and Wham (Richard Cary
File No.: Morgan PL-10222 RG 6p653A-43908, Langhammer
Cause No.: 76-LM-353 Circuit Court Madison County
Summary: Date of Accident: 3/14/1975. Products case involving 1974 Chevy Camaro. Rural Rt. 2, Pocahontas, IL. Plaintiff claims steering mechanism failed causing him to swerve off of road and strike concrete wall.

RUHLING, WILLIAM v ILLINI FEDERAL v ACORN ALUMINUM PRODUCTS, et al (Royal-Globe)
Amount of Suit: $10,000.00
Attorney: P- Tom O'Donnell; Illini Fed.-Allen Churchill
File No.: W653A - Wisdom
Cause No.: 73-L-1640 Circuit Court St. Clair County
Set for Trial: RUHLIN
Summary: Date of Accident: 7/3/1971. Travelodge Motel, 1203 W More Drive, Marion, IL. Plaintiff walked through glass sliding doors and sues Illini Federal, the owner motel. Illini Federal filed third party complaint against Acorn Dist. Co, the installer of the glass doors.

DIESTELHORST, LOLA F. v GENERAL MOTORS CORP. et al
Amount of Suit: $15,000.00
Attorney: Smith, Allen, Moorman, Larson & Stalker
File No.: PL-10966 - Collins
Cause No.: 76-L-847 Circuit Court Madison County
Summary: Date of Accident: 12/14/1974. Products liability case involving 1974 Oldsmobile. Macoupin Street, Gillespie, IL. Plaintiff was walking along street and claims gearshift jumped from "park" to "drive" causing car to lurch forward and strike her.

HENDERICKSON, MAE v COACHMAN OIL COMPANY et al
(Northwestern National)
Amount of Suit: $25,000.00
Attorney: Mateyka and Hill
File No.: 32-2282 - Brown
Cause No.: 75-L-395 Circuit Court Madison County
Summary: Date of Accident: 12/31/1973. 2:45 PM, DJ's premises at 1151 Edwardsville Rd., Granite City, IL. Plaintiff silpped and fell in snow.

MAHLANDT, LAVERNE v DON SCHUBERT, et al
(Northwestern National)
Amount of Suit: $100,000.00
Attorney: Callis, Schooley, Fillcoff and Hartman
File No.: 29-7800 - Brown
Cause No.: 75L-746 Circuit Court Madison County
Summary: Date of Accident: 8/4/1975. Scaffold Act case. Co-defendant, Joy Mfg. Co., owner of building at Mt. Vernon, IL. Defendant is general contractor. Plaintiff, an ironworker, is employee of Orco Erection Co. Plaintiff fell from scaffold.

MARLETTE, LARRY A. v GENERAL MOTORS CORPORATION, et al
(Royal-Globe)
Amount of Suit: $100,000.00
Attorney: Chapman and Chapman (Charles)
File No.: PL-10051-Pinto
Cause No.: 74-L-776 Circuit Court Madison County
Summary: Date of Accident: 3/7/1974. Plaintiff claims Defendant disposed of barrels of corrosive material and Plaintiff was injured when he came in contact with the material.

MUNTON, TAYLOR v CENTRAL ILLINOIS PUBLIC SERVICE CO v KNAACK MANUFACTURING CO, et al (Commercial Union)
Amount of Suit: $25,000.00
Attorney: P-Paul Storment Jr.;
                   CIPS-Droste and Droste (Larry Price)
File No.:   Wilde
Cause No.:   75-L-9 Circuit Court Montogmery County
Summary: Date of Accident: 2/23/1975. 3:00 AM at CIPS plant at Coffeen, IL. Plaintiff injured by toolbox and sues CIPS for negligence. CIPS sues Knaack for indemnity because Knaack manufactured toolbox.

LITTLE, ALEXANDRE v GENERAL MOTORS CORPORATION (Royal-Globe)
Amount of Suit: $15,000.00
Attorney: James Gomric
File No.:   XR653A-26858 - Wisdom
Cause No.:   74-L-2453 Circuit Court St. Clair County
Summary: Date of Accident: 5/16/1973. Products Liability case. 1974 Olds Toronado. Plaintiff driving his car at State St., E. St. Louis, rear ended automobile in front forcing it into other automobile. Plaintiff claims that brakes failed.

PREDIGER, LEIGH ANN, etc. v GENERAL MOTORS CORPORATION et al (Royal-Globe)
Amount of Suit: $2,100,000.00
Attorney: C E Heiligenstein
File No.:   PL-09755-June Morgan
Cause No.:   75-L-3684 Circuit Court St. Clair County
Summary: Date of Accident: 10/11/1975. Products Liability case involving 1974 Chevrolet pickup. Plaintiff claims defective brakes, wheel shields and shock absorbers and that rocks lodged between shields and brakes and front wheels. Plaintiff, a passenger in truck driven by Co-defendant Peteres, on Caspers Rd., Washington County, IL. Truck ran off road and overturned.

BATH, MARGARET v GENERAL MOTORS CORPORATION & CARL FOCHT
(Royal-Globe)
Amount of Suit: $200,000.00
Attorney: John E. Norton
File No.:   R653A-17436 - Roach
Cause No.:   70-3454 Circuit Court St. Clair County
Summary: Date of Accident: 3/14/1969. Chevrolet Plant, St. Louis, MO. Plaintiff, an inspector, injured her hand in a conveyor belt.

CINCEBOX, CHARLES v STRONG-LITE PRODUCT CO., et al v EXXON
Attorney: P-Thoms Lakin; D-Joe Davidson
Cause No.:   75-L-847
Summary: Plaintiff sustained eye injury.

SEEHAUSEN, CHARLES J. et al v SCHRIMPF, MARK
(Northwestern Nationa)
Amount of Suit: Count I - $500,000; Count II $30,000
Attorney: Dick Mudge
File No.:   32-2504 - D - Brown
Cause No.:   75-L-158 Circuit Court Madison County
Summary: Date of Accident: 12/20/1974. 11:50 PM, Mark IV Service Station, 3690 E. Broadway, Alton, IL. Plaintiff accidently shot with a Smith & Wesson Magnum 44 pistol.

MORIARITY, PATRICK C. v GENERAL MOTORS CORP. et al
(Royal-Globe)
Amount of Suit: $50,000.00
Attorney: Smith, Allen, Moorman, Larson & Lakin
File No.: PL-09812 (M) Morgan
Summary: Date of Accident: 11/15/1973. Products Liability case involving 1974 Chevrolet. Plaintiff claims car had defective seat belt lock. 11:17 AM in front of 1820 Vandalia St., Collinsville, IL. Plaintiff north on Vandalia rear ended by Co-Defendant.

MOORE, CURTIS for the use and benefit of State Farm Mutual Auto Insurance Co. v GENERAL MOTORS, et al
Amount of Suit: $2,270.92
Attorney: Brady, Donovan and Hatch - Nester
Cause No.: 77-LM-3702 Circuit Court St. Clair County
Summary: Plaintiff claims brakes malfunctioned causing Plaintiff to lose control and strike a light pole.

LOWDER, JOHN D. v GENERAL MOTORS CORP.
Attorney: P-Cox & Bassett;
D Gibson - Hoagland, Maucker, etc.;
Sunderland-Bernard & Davidson
File No.: ON 653 A 30376 - GM PL12879 Collins
Cause No.: 75-L-71 Jerseyville, IL.
Summary: Date of Accident: 10/18/1973. 4:20 PM State St., Jerseyville, IL. Defendant, driving 1972 Chevrolet in northerly direction on State St. was being approached by Plaintiff Lowder opearting a Honda motorcycle. Gibson started to turn left and claims accelerator stuck. When he attempted to pull back he collided with Plaintiffs approaching motorcycle.

CAIN, FLOYD A. v GENERAL MOTORS CORP. (Royal-Globe)
Amount of Suit: $9,000.00
Attorney: Chapman & Chapman (Gary Peel)
File No.:   PL-10722-Collins
Cause No.:   76-LM-780 Circuit Court Madison County
Summary: Date of Accident: 4/13/1976. Products Liability case.
1976 Oldsmobile 98 Regency. Carlyle, IL. Plaintiff's automobile burst into flames and burned.

ROBINSON, ELBRIDGE v INTERNATIONAL HARVESTER CO.
(Royal-Globe)
Amount of Suit: $1,000,000.00
Attorney: Kassly, Weihl and Bone, Carlson
File No.:   Heim
Cause No.:   72-1054 Circuit Court St. Clair County
Summary: Products Liability case. Plaintiff claims he was injured while operating an International Pay Loader H-25B.

PIESZCHALSKI, DEBORA, Conservator of the Estate of Mark A., an incompetent person v INTERNATIONAL HARVESTER CO. (Esis-Miller)
Amount of Suit: $5,000,000.00
Attorney: C E Heiligenstein
File No.:   ESIS NO. 560 (Miller) (Trinley)
Cause No.:   78-L-368 Circuit Court St. Clair County
Summary: Date of Accident: 10/24/1977. Intersection of Waltonville-Ashley Rd. & Hall Rd. in Washington County. Plaintiff operating automobile in northerly direction on Waltonville-Ashley Rd. when he collided with Co-Defendant's westbound IH 560 tractor being operated in a westerly direction on Hall Rd. Plaintiff alleges that the tractor was unreasonably dangerous because it contained no reflectors or lights to warn approaching motorists after sunrise or before sunset.

INDIAN HEAD, INC. v THE CALUMITE COMPANY
(See also: Amberly v St. Lous Slag)
Amount of Suit: $275,000.00
Attorney: Roberts, Gundlach & Lee
File No.: Victor Bryand, Jr.
Cause No.: 71-88 Federal Court East St. Louis
Summary: Plaintiff's Lincoln, IL plant purchased calumite slag to be used in making glass and claims it was defective. The product was used over a period of time from 8/27/68 through 1/69.

HOPKINS, R.W. et al d/b/a AMBERLEY PARTNERSHIP v ST. LOUIS SLAG PRODUCTS COMPANY, INC. (See also Indian head v Calumite)
Amount of Suit: $715,437.46
Attorney: Victor Bryant - Durham, NC
Cause No.: Circuit Court Madison County
Summary: Breach of contract action. Contract breached on August 8, 1969.

MILLER, DOROTHY, Admr. v GENERAL MOTORS CORP.
(Royal-Globe)
Amount of Suit: $100,000.00
Attorney: Harry J. Sterling
File No.: Morgan - PL-10297
Cause No.: 76-L-370 Circuit Court Madison County
Summary: Date of Accident: 8/29/1975. 12:20 PM I-50 near Bayless Rd. in St. Louis County, MO. Wrongful death case involving 1974 Chevrolet Model 30 Step-Van. Deceased was driving van when he collided with something and was thrown from van. Seatbelt had been removed from driver's seat to be used at helper's stand. Plaintiff claims van was defective because it did not have seatbelt.

McCRAY, DAVID v CALVERT, VIRGIL, et al
(Northwestern National)
Amount of Suit: $25,000.00
Attorney: Edward Neville
File No.:   29-7903-Brown
Cause No.:   75-:-2836 Circuit Court St. Clair County
Summary: Date of Accident: 8/1/1973. 2600 Lake Drive. Plaintiff, riding bicycle, collided with vehicle driven by Defendant.

GRIMES, OPAL v COUGHENOUR, ALLEN A. (Plaintiff Case)
Amount of Suit: $150,000.00
Attorney: Evans and Dixon (Ralph Kleinschmidt)
Cause No.:   363463 Division I, Circuit Court St. Louis County
Summary: Date of Accident: 4/3/1973. Defendant extracted impacted wisdom teetn resulting in injury to nerve in Plaintiff's face.

RYAN, EVERETT et al v INTERNATIONAL HARVESTER
(Royal-Globe)
Amount of Suit: $750,000.00
Attorney: C.E. Heiligenstein
File No.:   Wisdom- 653A-35374
Cause No.:   74-L-2797 Circuit Court St. Clair County
Summary: Date of Accident: 8/11/1974. Products Liability Case involving 1965 International Travel-Al. Douglas-Millstadt Rd. & Floraville Rd. Plaintiff's in Travel-All east on Douglas-Millstadt Rd. collided with Co-Defendant north on Floraville Rd. Travel-All caught fire.

TAYLOR, MILTON R. v OUTBOARD MARINE CORP. et al
(Commercial Union)
Attorney: C.E. Heiligenstein
File No.: Wilde
Cause No.: 77-L-2488 Circuit Court St. Clair County
Summary: Date of Accident: 3/12/1975. Products Liability case involving Cushman Commerical gasoline cart. General Tire and Rubber Co, Mt. Vernon, IL. Plaintiff, riding on cart, was thrown from cart when it turned suddenly.

VIVIANO, PEGGY v PETER BARTSCH, MD et al
(Commercial Union)
Amount of Suit: $250,000.00
Attorney: Bruce Cook;
Searle Corp.-Burton Bernard;
Mead Johnson-Schwarz
File No.: K4-9975 Hoerath
Cause No.: 75-L-207 Circuit Court Madison County
Summary: Malpractice case. Plaintiff claims she was given oral contraceptives by Defendant and later developed thrombophlebitis.

BLAKE, HERBERT v MYERS INDUSTRIES, INC. et al
(Commercial Union)
Amount of Suit: $400,000.00
Attorney: Pratt, Kardis, Pierce & Bradford
File No.: Wilde
Cause No.: 75-L-120 Circuit Court Madison County
Summary: Date of Accident: 7/23/1975. Scaffold Act case. Near Jacksonville, IL.

SAMOTIS, JOHN Admr. v GENERAL MOTORS CORPORATION et al
(Royal-Globe)
Amount of Suit: $100,000.00
Attorney: John E. Norton
File No.: R 653 A-16767-English
Cause No.: Civ. 70-3408 Circuit Court St. Clair County
Summary: Date of Accident: 4/26/1969. 9:30 PM, US Hwy 460 at Route 13, St. Clair County, IL. Wrongful death case. Plaintiff and deceased wife traveling west on 460 passed mail truck and thereafter collided with concrete overhead abutment. Plaintiff claims defective steering on 1969 Oldsmobile caused accident

DAVIDSON, MARVIN L. v ILLINOIS CENTAL GULF RR CO & PULLMAN INCORPORATED
Amount of Suit: Count II, IV, V - $200.000.00
Attorney: P-Kassly, Bone, Becker & Carlson;
Co-Defendant Freeark, Harvey & Mendilllo
File No.: Bill Marshall
Cause No.: 76-L-3741 Circuit Court St. Clair County
Summary: Date of Accident: 5/2/1976. Venice Yards of ICG RR. Plaintiff, an employee of Universal Leaseway System of Illinois, Inc., claims he was actually working for the ICG. While he was assisting in loading a semi-trailer onto a flat bed car and while under the trailer the stanchion to a hitch supporting the front of the trailer failed causing Plaintiff to jump and injure himself. Plaintiff claims that Pullman manufactured the hitch.

MATHES, SHELBY RaY v GENERAL MOTORS CORPORATION
(Royal -Globe)
Amount of Suit: $300,000.00
Attorney: Goldenhersh & Goldenhersh (Mike Katz)
File No.: OP653A31229-00 Temple
Cause No.: 74-L-1443 Circuit Court St. Clair County

POLITO, ANTHONY v J.J. ALTMAN & CO.
(Northwestern National)
Amount of Suit: $40,000.00
Attorney: Jerome Schlichter - Cohn, Carr
File No.: 82-2207 Brown
Cause No.: 71-2846
Summary: Date of Accident: 7/5/1971. Near Scott Air Force Base. Construction job accident. We are only observers in this case at the present time.

MATTHEWS, RITA v INTERNATIONAL et al
Amount of Suit: $100,000.00
Attorney: P-Champan; Pic-n-Puff-Maushcer; Revlon-Lesker; Jaeger-Bertrand; Morris-Burt Bernard
File No.: K4-6959-Wilde
Cause No.: 73-L-71 Circuit Court Madison County
Summary: Plaintiff, having hair frosted, sustained burns.

BETTS, DONALD E and THOMAS v GENERAL MOTORS, et al
(Royal-Globe)
Amount of Suit: Less than $10,000.00
Attorney: Bob Larson
File No.: GM PL-12602
Cause No.: 78-LM-378
Summary: Date of Accident: 10/7/1977. Shipman Rd., Madison County. Plaintiff, operating pickup truck in southerly direction on Shipman Rd. when he was struck by Co-Defendant approaching in 1967 Chevelle 2-door. Plaintiff claims the Chevelle went out of control and crossed the centerline becuase of a defective idler arm, steering assembly and brake drum.

HUNTER, GARY v GENERAL MOTORS et al
Amount of Suit: Excess of $15,000.
Attorney: C.T. Ducey, Sr.
Cause No.:   77-L-3325 Circuit Court St. Clair County
Summary: Date of Accident: 10/27/1976. Alleged personal injuries due to defective dump truck manufactured by GM when unreasonably dangerous power take-off disengaged without warning.

LANE, SHIRLEY, Admr. v McCABE-POWERS BODY CO.
(Lord, Bissell & Brook)
Amount of Suit: $500,000.00
Attorney: Ted Harvey
Cause No.:   77-L-4474 Circuit Court St. Clair County
Summary: Larry Lane, an employee of Southeastern IL Electric Cooperative, Inc., was part of a crew trimming a tree in Franklin County, Benton, IL when boom was caused to come into contact with electric power line causing death.

GIESELMANN, LISA GAY v PEABODY COAL COMPANY et al
(Old Republic Insurance Companies)
Amount of Suit: $15,000.00
Attorney: Ducey and Feder
Cause No.:   79-L0171 Circuit Court St. Clair County
Summary: Date of Accident: 12/11/1978. Intersection of Gravel Rd. and the Peabody Coal Mine entrance in Randolph County.

KORINEK, L. & SON CO. v SALVAGE & BRIDGES AGENCy, INC. et al
(Northwestern National)
Amount of Suit: $30,000.00
Attorney: Meyer & Kaucher
File No.: 82-2852-D-Brown
Cause No.: 76-L-162 Circuit Court Madison County
Summary: Suit for breach of oral contract and negligence in not providing proper insurance coverage.

SHAW, VIRGIL v GENERAL MOTORS et al
(Royal-Globe)
Amount of Suit: $500,000.00
Attorney: Hillebrand, Cook & Shevlin
File No.: 4P653A-40835 - Wisdom
Cause No.: 75-L-3090 Circuit Court St. Clair County
Summary: Date of Accident: 10/30/1973. Products Liability case involving 1973 Chevrolet Tandem truck. Plaintiff injured while working on construction job when truck backed over him. Plaintiff claims truck should have been equipped with back-up bell.

STEED, ROONEY E. et al v GENERAL MOTORS CORP
(Royal-Globe)
Amount of Suit: $15,000.00
Attorney: freeark, Harvey & Mendillo
File No.: PL 13125 Collins
Cause No.: 78-L-795 Circuit Court St. Clair County
Summary: Date of Accident: 6/29/1978. Products Liability case involving 1976 GMC Chemical Spreader Model 6500. Oak and Main Streets, Hoyleton, IL. 10 year old Plaintiff, on bicycle, collided with the chemical spreader.

SODERLUND, MICHAEL E. et al v DATSUN MOTOR CORPORATION d/b/a NISSAN MOTOR CORPORATION IN USA
Amount of Suit: Excess of $15,000.
Attorney: Norton-Bonifield
Cause No.:   81-L-101 Circuit Court St. Clair County
Summary: Date of Accident: 6/8/1979. Products Liability case involving Datsun automobile. 5:35 PM at intersection of Rt. 121 and 98 in Tazewell County, IL. Plaintiff's were passengers in northbound Datsun on Rt. 121 when it made left turn onto Rt. 98. Datsun was struck by southbound truck on Rt. 121. Plaintiff's claim that seats of Datsun and seatbelts were inadequate.

HANEY, VIRGINIA etc. v GENERAL MOTORS et al
(Royal-Globe)
Amount of Suit: Excess of $15,000.
Attorney: L. Thomas Lakin (Gary Peel)
File No.:   Doug Brown - 19734
Cause No.:   79-L-356 Circuit Court Madison County
Summary: Date of Accident: 5/1/1978. Plaintiff decedent, Roy Haney) operating 1973 GMC Sierra on McAdams Pkwy. (Great River Rd.) about 200 feet east of Norman's Landing in Madison County. Plaintiff claims that the vehicle left the roadway due to a defective steering mechanism, braking system, and accelration system. In an earlier Dram Shop Count, Plaintiff alleges that Haney's vehicle left the road becuase he was drunk.

POWDEN, GERALD E & HELEN B. LUTZ v CHEVROLET MOTOR DIVISION, GENERAL MOTORS CORP. (Royal-Globe)
Amount of Suit: Count I-excess of $15,000.00;
Count II- excess of $10,000.00
Attorney: Listeman, Bandy & Hamilton
File No.: GM 20204 Parshall
Cause No.: 80L-529 Circuit Court St. Clair County
Summary: Date of Accident: 8/11/1979. Plaintiff Lutz purchased automobile, 1979 Chevrolet Monte Carlo, on 8/16/79. At 1:44 PM, when automobile had approximately 200 miles on it, accident occurred. Auto was westbound on I-64 with cruise control in operation and traveling at approximately 55 MPH. Plaintiff intended to exit I-64 at 159 and as she drove onto the exit ramp she applied her brakes. Instead of the auto slowing down, it sped up and she ultimately crossed the median and came to rest in a field.

RUBY, IVAN v CONTINENTAL BOILER WORKS, INC. et al
(Commercial Union)
Amount of Suit: $2,000,000.00
Attorney: Schooley
File No.: Wilde
Cause No.: 75-L-730 Circuit Court Madison County
Summary: Date of Accident: 2/4/1975. Plaintiff, employed by AMEX, injured at their plant at Sauget. Plaintiff entered "Lurgi Roaster" to remove slag and was burned.

ROBERTSON, KENNETH E. etc. v WHITE FARM EQUIPMENT Co. et al
(See also Bass v Rincker)
Amount of Suit: $20,000.00 plus costs
Attorney: Leon Scroggins; Thomas F. Londrigan
Cause No.: 78-L-587 Circuit Court Madison County
Summary: Date of Accident: 11/19/1976. Plaintiff's decedent was a passenger in the Bass auto when it hit the rear end of a farm wagon manufactured by White Farm Equipment Co. sold by Sears and driven by Chester D. Horn.

A/S RAUFOSS v OLIN CORPORATION
Amount of Suit: $2,000,000.00
Attorney: P-Lewis, Rice, Tucker, Allen & Chubb;
Hale Russell & Gray;
Mateyka, Hill, Hill & Armstrong
Cause No.: USDC Southern Distrrict #81-3343
Summary: Suit is based upon alleged breach of warranty, breach of contract, misrepresentation, negligence and strict liability in tort.

PHILLIPS, JOHN E. v JEEP CORPORATION, et al RUETHER'S INVETMENT COMPANY d/b/a REUTHER JEEP SALES
Amount of Suit: $6M-Compensatory & $10M punitive
Attorney: P-Carpel & Bourey; Jeep Corp.-Hatch
Cause No.: 80-5083 USDC Southern District, Alton
Summary: Date of Accident: 4/11/1979. Plaintiff, a passenger in a 1975 Jeep CJ-5 operated by Robert Olesen in a northerly direction on N. Oakland Ave. Jeep was stuck by another auto being driven by Mary Hanstedt after which the Jeep rolled over. Plaintiff thrown from Jeep. Plaintiff claims Jeep was defectively designed.

PARR, MARTIN STEVE etc. v GENERAL MOTORS CORP.
(Royal-Globe)
Amount of Suit: Excess of $15,000.
Attorney: James P. Newcomb
Cause No.: 566-79 Circuit Court Sangamon County
Summary: Date of Accident: 7/5/1979. Products Liability case involving 1972 Buick Skylark. Plaintiff claims that while he was attempting to "jump" the Dura-start Big Shot Model 74-6MF battery, the battery exploded in Plaintiff's face.

JOHNSON, SAYERS, et al v U-HAUL COMPANY, et al
Amount of Suit: Count I-$25,000.00; Punitive-$5,000,000.00
Attorney: Rex Carr
File No.:   Mike Shoen
Cause No.:   74-L-3125 Circuit Court St. Clair County
Summary: Date of Accident: 8/25/1973. 5:10 PM - I-44 (US66) near Waynesville, MO. Plaintiff's westbound with U-Haul trailer. Lost control and injured.

ELLERMEYER, ROSIE, Admr. v GENERAL MOTORS CORP. et al
(Royal-Globe)
Amount of Suit: $100,000.00
Attorney: Goldenhersh & Goldenhersh (Del Goldenhersh)
File No.:   PL-10634 IS-IL - Collins
Cause No.:   76-L-3063 Circuit Court St. Clair County
Summary: Date of Accident: 8/21/1975. Wrongful death case. Products Liability case involving 1975 Chevrolet Fleetside pickup truck. Decedent, driving truck on IL Rt. 34, 8 miles east of IL Rt. 37 in Franklin County, IL, when tire falied causing truck to overturn.

COX, HAROLD v GENERAL MOTORS CORP.
(Royal-Globe)
Amount of Suit: $150,000.00
Attorney: Talbert & Fitzgerald (Mallon)
File No.:   653-A-35376 Watts
Cause No.:   75-L-257 Circuit Court Madison County
Summary: Date of Accident: 9/25/1974. Products Liability case involving 1974 Buick Century. Rt. 140 near Alton State Hospital, Alton, IL. Plaintiff, driving automobile, claims he ran off highway due to bad steering.

HANEY, CLARICE A Admin. Etc. v CLIFFORD, L. BELL and JOHN A. DURHAM (Commercial Union)
Amount of Suit: $100,000.00
Attorney: C.E. Heiligenstein
File No.: WG 818970 - Held
Cause No.: 79-L-1049 Circuit Court St. Clair County
Summary: Date of Accident: 11/2/1979. Wrongful death case. Intersection of Route 3 and Bypass 50, Monroe County, IL. Deceased, a passenger in Defendant's southbound auto on Rt. 3 when it collided with Co-Defendant's eastbound truck on Rt. 50.

MACK, CALLIE v. GENERAL MOTORS CORP. et al
Attorney: Ducey and Feder (Neil Ducey)
File No.: PL-08232; PL-09271 - Collins
Cause No.: 75-L-529 Circuit Court Madison County
Summary: Products Liability case involving 1974 Chevrolet Caprice. Death action. Decedent driving north on I-55 near Glenarm, IL when his car caught on fire. Decedent stopped his car beside pavement and as he was walking across highway he was struck and killed by a tractor trailer truck

HOPKINS, HAZEL v.FULTS et al FARMERS & MERCHANTS BANK OF HIGHLAND v FULTS et al (Empire Insurance Co)
Amount of Suit: Excess of $15,000.
Attorney: Ducey & Feder
File No.: Policy #BA-709490
Cause No.: Hopkins-78-L-955;
Farmers-79-L-148 Circuit Court St. Clair County
Summary: Date of Accident: 10/25/1978. 3:45 PM on US Rt. 50 near Carlyle Lake Rd. in Carlyle, IL. Spence Heywood operating tractor-trailer truck in westerly direction on Rt. 50. Co-Defendant Schaubert drove onto Rt. 50 from Carlyle Lake Rd. in front of Heywood's truck. Heywood's truck collided with Schaubert's vehicle and then collided with Hopkins vehicle.

DAVIDSON, MARVIN L. v PULLMAN INCORPORATED, et al
Amount of Suit: $500,000.00
Attorney: Maurice Bone
File No.: Bertram Beers - William Marshall
Cause No.: 78-L-492 Circuit Court St. Clair County
Summary: Date of Accident: 5/11/1978. 2:00 or 3:00 PM at the ICG Yards in E. St. Louis, IL on Track #1. Plaintiff was setting brake on backend of piggyback car TTX477688 when it slipped or jerked causing him to fall backwards.

PULLAM, EVERETT L. v GENERAL MOTORS CORPORATION, et al
Amount of Suit: Excess of $15,000.
Attorney: William S. Schildman
Cause No.: 79-L-3 Circuit Court Scott County, Winchester, IL
Summary: Date of Accident: 2/17/1977. Plaintiff's 1975 Chevy van collided with horse on Highway 100 one mile north of Bluffs, Scott County, IL. Plaintiff claims he was injured because the mounting brackets on the steering column extended down into the passenger area.

REDDING, RANDALL H. et ux v GENERAL MOTORS CORPORATION, et al
(Royal-Globe - Springfield, IL-Franchis Koehler)
Amount of Suit: $10,000.00
Attorney: Hart, Hart and Gulley
File No.: PL-12838-Collins
Cause No.: 78-LM-94 Circuit Court Franklin County, Benton, IL
Summary: Date of Accident: 3/14/1977. 8:30 PM on Highway 14, 2 miles east of US Highway 51 in Perry County, IL. Plaintiff claims that as he was driving the truck the steering mechanism locked and the truck ran off the highway into a drainage ditch.

BASS, LYNETTE ANN, et al v WHITE FARM EQUIPMENT Co., et al
(Rooks, Pitts Fullagar & Poust) (See also Robertson v White Farm Equipment
& Rincker v White Farm Equipment)
Amount of Suit: $50,000.00 + $5,000 funeral expenses
Attorney: C.E. Heiligenstein
Cause No.: 78-L-209 Circuit Court St. Clair County
Summary: Date of Accident: 11/19/1976. Plaintiff's decedent drove his auto into the rear-end of a farm wagon manufactured by White Farm Equipment, sold by Sears and driven by Chester D. Horn.

SMITH, SIDNEY E. and BANK OF PONTIAC, Admr. Of Estate of Joseph R. Snell, deceased v GENERAL MOTORS CORPORATION and SUMMA CORPORATION (Associated Aviation Underwriters)
Attorney: Jerom Mirza & Associates
File No.: LM-982 - Henry W. Taffe,
Assoc. Aviation Underwriters
Cause No.: 786-78 Circuit Court, 7th Judicial Circuit,
Sangamon County
Set for Trial: 12/11/1976
Summary: Date of Accident: 12/11/1976. Products liability case involving a helicopter crash. Helicopter manufactured by Hughes Helicopter Div. of Summa Corp. The turbine was manufactured by Detroit Diesel Allison Div. of GMC at Indianapolis, IN. Plaintiff Smith flying the helicopter when it crashed in Livingston County, IL. Smith injured. Passenger Joseph R. Snell ws killed

RINCKER, GAIL et al v WHITE FARM EQUIPMENT Co., et al (Rooks, Pitts Fullagar & Poust) (See Bass v White Farm Equip & Robertson v. White Farm Equip.)
Amount of Suit: Excess of $15,000.
Attorney: Owen, Roberts, Susler & Murphy (Darrell Parish)
File No.: Wayne Plaza
Cause No.: 78-L-26 Circuit Court Shelbyville, IL
Summary: Date of Accident: 11/19/1976. 6:00 PM on County Line blacktop road one mile SW of Cowden, IL. Plaintiff's traveling south struck by northbound vehicle driven by Bass after it struck farm wagon owned by Horn.

BLAINE, BARBARA E. v GENERAL MOTORS CORPORATION
(Royal-Globe)
Amount of Suit: $1,000,000.00
Attorney: Wiseman, Shaikewitz, McGivern & Wahl
File No.: PL-12950-Collins
Cause No.: 78-5159-USDC Southern District (Alton)
Summary: Date of Accident: 5/28/1977. Products Liability case. Accident occurred at 7:30 PM near 2627 Thomas, Alton, IL. Plaintiff, operating dune buggy when it overturned. Plaintiff claims her seatbelt came loose.

BRAUE, JOHN v VOLKSWAGEN, et al
Amount of Suit: $100,000.00
Attorney: Mateyka and Hill
File No.: 24-J06312 - Arentzen
Cause No.: 76-L-230 Circuit Court Madison County
Summary: Date of Accident: 5/10/1975. Products Liability case involivng 1972 VW Beetle. 2:30 AM, Route 157 near Edwards. Plaintiff's deceased eastbound in Beetle struck head-on by Co-Defendant.

REICHLING, STEVEN v PEABODY COAL COMPANY & TOM AMOS
Amount of Suit: $1,266.42
Attorney: Ross T. Andeson
File No.:   936707 Old Republic Co.
Cause No.:   81-SC-1026 Circuit Court St. Clair County
Summary: Date of Accident: 7/7/1980. Peabody vehicle being drive by Tom Amos rolled backwards into the front of Plaintiff's vehicle.

BIEBER, ELMER J. v GENERAL MOTORS CORPORATION, et al
(Royal-Globe)
Amount of Suit: $15,000.00
Attorney: Tom D. Adams
File No.:   Wisdom 9P653A52829 - Collins
Cause No.:   77-L-4209 Circuit Court St. Clair County
Summary: Date of Accident: 10/12/1976. 2:50 PM at intersection of IL State Route 3 and US Bypass 50 in Columbia, IL. Plaintiff, northbound on Route 3, was stopped at red light at intersection with US Bypass 50. While stopped he was rear ended by 1974 Chevy semi-tractor truck being operated by Co-Defendant, Forest Vickery, while engaged in his employement for Co-Defendant Niederbrach Truck Service. Inc.

SELIKSON, MARK H. v U-Haul, et al
Amount of Suit: Count I -$200,000.00; Count II 200,000.00; Count III $5,000,000.00
Attorney: Rex Carr
File No.:   Baxter
Cause No.:   76-L-1789 Circuit Court St. Clair County
Summary: Date of Accident: 6/12/1975. 10:28 AM on I-55 north of Springfield. Plaintiff, traveling south in 1961 Willy's Jeep pulling four wheel U-Haul ATV trailer. Plaintiff drove onto right hand shoulder causing trailer to fish-tail and eventually hit bridge abutment

BRANSTETTER, GAYLA v U-HAUL COMPANY and Clarence Coddington dba Coddington Oil Co. aka Coddington Service Station (Republic Claims Service Co.)
Amount of Suit: $15,000.00
Attorney: Listeman, Bandy and Hamiton
File No.:   05-526155
Cause No.:   79-L-118 Circuit Court St. Clair County
Summary: Date of Accident: 3/13/1978. Near West Plains, MO. Plaintiff rented a U-Haul truck from Coddington Oil Co. in St. Clair County. Plaintiff intended to move to Mountain Home, AR. Plaintiff claims that the engine blew up causing the truck to veer off the highway.

GIBSON, JOE S v PEABODY COAL COMPANY, et al
(Old Republic Companies)
Amount of Suit: $100,000.00
Attorney: C.E. Heiligenstein
Cause No.:   78-L501 Circuit Court St. Clair County
Summary: Date of Accident: 3/6/1978. Peabody's River King Mine at Freeburg, IL. Plaintiff, an inspector for US was riding as a passenger on an underground personnel carrier when it collided head-on with an underground locomotive.

FIELDS, JOHN J. Admr. Of estates of Kathleen Fields, deceased, and John C. Fields, deceased v AMERICAN SHEET AND STRIP STEEL, INC., et al
Attorney: Wm. Schooley
Cause No.:   78-L-972 Circuit Court Madison County
Summary: Date of Accident: 12/22/1976. 5:10 PM on IL Route 162 in Madison County. Plaintiff's, in Volkswagen westbound on IL 162 when it was rear-ended by Co-Defedendant. Plaintiff Fields injured, wife and son killed.

ALTON AND SOUTHERN RAILWAY COMPANY v ALTON
TRANSPORTATION COMPANY et al (Kortenhof)
Amount of Suit: $100,000.00
Attorney: Walker and Williams (Sterling)
Cause No.:   74-L-1515 Circuit Court St. Clair County
Summary: Date of Accident: 1/12/1973. Barges fleeted by Notre Dame Fleeting and Towing Service broke loose and struck the Fox Terminal dock of Plaintiff.

EVERS, WILLIAM v COACHMAn OIL COMPANY, et al
(Northwestern National Insurance Co.)
Amount of Suit: $300,000.00
Attorney: Bertrand, Bauman and Schmeider
Cause No.:   73-2348 Circuit Court St. Clair County
Summary: Date of Accident: 6/12/1972. 8:30 AM at Defendant's service station at 1151 Edws. Rd., Granite City, IL. Plaintiff, a painter, fell from scaffold while engaged in painting Defendant's service station.

JONES, HAROLD B., Admr. v NORFOLK AND WESTERN RR CO.
Amount of Suit: $50,000.00
Attorney: Cohn, Carr et al (Lakin)
File No.:   L-12642 - Sample
Cause No.:   73 L 35 Circuit Court Madison County
Summary: Date of Accident: 2/22/1972. Wrongful death case. 4:45 PM at the Wolf St. grade crossing in Edws, IL. Plaintiff, west on Wolf St., struck by southbound train.

HURST, HENRY v GENERAL MOTORS CORPORATION
(Royal -Globe) (See Griffin v General Motors)
Amount of Suit: $500,000.00
Attorney: Wiseman, Shaikewitz, etc.
File No.:   R653A 23359 Wisdom
Cause No.:   S Civ-72-173 USDC Southern District, Springfield, IL
Summary: Date of Accident: 10/20/1971. Drummondville, Quebec, Canada. Plaintiff, employee of Jack Grifin dba Fisherman's Paradise Lake. Griffin purchaed GMC truck and put a fish tank on it. Was transporting live fish. Plaintiff struck another vehice and lost control and went off into a ditch. Plaintiff claims accelerator stuck causing accident.

BREMEN, JOHN et al v EAST ST. LOUIS AND INTER-URBAN WATER COMPANY, et al (Royal-Globe)
Attorney: Thomas LeChien
File No.:   6R653A28955 - Temple
Cause No.:   73-L-1808 Circuit Court St. Clair County
Summary: Date of Accident: 1/1/1973. 2:30 AM at 1020 N. Belt West, Swansea, IL. Plaintiffs claim water company water line leaked causing water to accumulate and freeze on pavement causing automobile accident.

BEATTY, JOHN v. WALSTON AVIATION, INC. et al
(Royal-Globe)
Amount of Suit: $100,000.00
Attorney: Boman, Leskera & Churchill
Cause No.:   73-L-678 Circuit Court Madison County
Summary: Date of Accident: 1/15/1972. 1:00 PM Plaintiff fell over 1 foot high chain fence at airport. He slipped on ice on the sidewalk and then tripped into the fence and fell.

ALDRICH, WILBERTA A. v ELLIS W. LONG, et al
(Commercial Union)
Amount of Suit: $40,000.00
Attorney: Meyer and Kaucher
File No.:   K4-7047, Wilde
Cause No.:   73-L-636 Circuit Court Madison County
Set for Trial: 11/18/1974
Summary: Date of Accident: 6/26/1973. Rt. 4 near intersection with Rt. 40. Defendant in semi-truck rear ended Plaintiff.

HAKE, IMOGENE, Admr., v INTERNATIONAL HARVESTER, et al (Royal-Globe)
Amount of Suit: $250,000.00
Attorney: Wham and Wham
File No.:   S653A-22133 - Heim
Cause No.:   72-1067 Circuit Court St. Clair County
Summary: Date of Accident: 7/29/1971. Wrongful death case. 11:15 AM at Huegely, IL. Deceased was riding tractor being demonstrated when he fell of, was run over by the tractor and killed.

BOSSING, THERESA, a minor, etc. v AMERICAN WELDING MFG. CO., et al (Commercial Union)
Amount of Suit: $30,000.00
Attorney: Smith, Allen & Moorman
File No.:   K4-6297 - Wilde
Cause No.:   73-L-378
Summary: Date of Accident: 5/16/1972. 9:30 AM Plaintiff, a student at Collinsville school, was exiting thorugh metal doors and injured.

HARRIS, LIZZIE B. v DR. CHARLES R. FRAZER, et al
(Commercial Union)
Amount of Suit: $200,000.00
Attorney: Hillebrand, Cook & Shevlin
File No.:   McWilliams
Cause No.:   73-L-2267
Summary: Date of Accident: 6/14/1972. Malpractice case. Plaintiff operated on by Defendant at St. Mary's Hospital for tumor on thyroid gland. Planitiff claims that vocal chords were severed.

NICHOLS, GERALD v 7302 Corporation, et al v W.R. SCHILLER CONSTRUCTION COMPANY (Employers Commerical Union)
Amount of Suit: $25,000.00
Attorney: O'Connell and Waller
File No.:   K4-4830 - McWilliams
Cause No.:   72-1017 Circuit Court St. Clair County
Summary: Date of Accident: 6/11/1970. Scaffold Act case. 7120 W. Main, Belleville, IL. Plaintiff, an ironworker employed by Mueller Erection, a sub of W.R. Schiller, was injured while engaged in building medical building for Defendant.

STAMM, REBECCA, a minor, etc. v HOLLIDAY ON WHEELS and GEORGE C. DEMETRULIAS, et al (Empire Insurance Co.)
Amount of Suit: $25,000.00
Attorney: Scott Richardson
File No.:   4-120735 - Reeves
Cause No.:   74-CIV-89 Circuit Court Monroe County (Waterloo)
Summary: Date of Accident: 3/9/1974. W.J. Zahnow School, Waterloo, IL. Defendant rented skates and equipment to PTA for skating party at school. Plaintiff fell and broke arm while skating.

BUTLER, EARL E., et al v DR. NORMAN L. CLAYBOURN, et al
(Commercial Union Assurance Co.)
Amount of Suit: $900,000.00
Attorney: Chapman and Chapman
File No.: K4 - Wilde
Cause No.: 72-L-167 Madison County
Summary: Date of Accident: 5/1/1971. Malpractice case. Plaintiff's claim they were injured because of Defendant's negligence while attending to them in the emergency room of St. Elizabeth's Hospital in Granite City, IL.

BUCHHOLZ, MARY M. v CARROLL, JOHN J., et al
(Commercial Union)
Amount of Suit: $150,000.00
Attorney: Chapman, Talbert and Chapman
File No.: K4-5688 - McWIlliams
Cause No.: 73-L-68 Circuit Court Madison County
Summary: Date of Accident: 11/26/1971. Malpractice case. Defendant performed hysterectomy on Plaintiff. Plaintiff subsequently developed a vesico-vaginal fistula.

VAN ETTEN, BENJAMIN, et al v CROWN CHEMICALS, INC.
(Northwestern National Insurance Co.)
Amount of Suit: $100,000.00
Attorney: Sam Xanders
File No.: 46-33352 - D Brown
Cause No.: 74-L-48 Circuit Court Madison County
Summary: Breach of contract action. Plaintiff marketed "X-Termite" manufactured by Defendant. Plaintiff claims that Defendant improperly made the product causing damage to Plaintiff's customers.

KLEIN, NANCY Lee, Admr. Etc. v INTERNATIONAL HARVESTER, et al
(Royal-Globe)
Amount of Suit: $250,000.00
Attorney: Crowder and Adams
File No.:   0S653A-28156 - Temple
Cause No.:   73-I-2675 Circuit Court St. Clair County
Summary: Date of Accident: 10/23/1971. Death case. 12:45 PM, Deceased, operating Model 3414 IH Loader Tractor on Peabody Coal property at New Athens, IL. Tractor overturned and killed deceased.

KIMBRO, JERALD v PARLANTE, V.J., et al
(Commercial Union)
Amount of Suit: $750,000.00
Attorney: Schooley and Hartman
File No.:   K4-666 - McWilliams
Cause No.:   72-M-415 Circuit Court Madison County
Summary: Date of Accident: 4/12/1972. Malpractice case. Plaintiff accidently shot self in right leg. Right leg eventually amputated.

FORE, LEO LAWRENCE, Adm. v EMPIRE STOVE, et al
(Safeco-General Insurance Co.)
Amount of Suit: Count I - $30,000.00; Count II - $1,500.00
Attorney: W.K. Kidwell; John Alan Appleman
File No.:   BLP209943 - Brinker
Cause No.:   65-2305 Circuit Court St. Clair County
Set for Trial: 4/17/1967
Summary: Date of Accident: 12/18/1963. Moweagua, IL. Wrongful death action. Plaintiff claims Paula Jean Denton asphyxiated by furnace manufactured by Defendant.

SETTLEMOIR, DAVID v TOWMOTOR CORPORATION v INDIANHEAD, INC. (Commercial Union Companies)
Amount of Suit: $50,000.00
Attorney: P - Tom LeChien; D - Robert Cadagin
File No.: K4-1217 McWilliams
Cause No.: 71-1162 District Court E. St. Louis
Summary: Date of Accident: 12/29/1969. 10:30 AM at Obear-Nester Plant, E. St. Louis. Plaintiff, operating Towmotor, injured when Towmotor ran into him. Plaintiff sues manufacturer who sues Obear-Nester.

JENKINS, KATHERINE v CENTRAL STATES CONFERENCE OF SEVENTH DAY ADVENTISTS, et al (Commercial Union) (See also National Auto & Casualty v Employers Commercial)
Amount of Suit: $10,000.00
Attorney: Lance Callis
File No.: K4-5534 Wilde
Cause No.: 72 M 447 Circuit Court Edwards Madison County
Summary: Date of Accident: 10/29/1971. Madison, IL. Plaintiff, traveling northon Madison Avenue, Defendant Morris driving west on 6th Street and collided. Issue is who had red light.

NATIONAL AUTOMOBILE & CASUALTY INSURANCE CO., et al v EMPLOYERS COMMERCIAL UNION INSURANCE CO., et al (Commercial Union) (See Jenkins v Morris, et al)
Amount of Suit: Declaratory judgment suit
Attorney: Wagner, Bertrand, Bauman & Schmieder
File No.: K4-5534 Wilde
Cause No.: 72-Z-153 Circuit Court Madison County
Summary: Date of Accident: 10/29/1971. DeElla Morris driving auto borrowed from Andrew Wilson in Madison and collided with auto driven by Katherine Jenkins. Wilson had no insurance. Morris working for Central States Conference of 7th Day Adventists. Employers has policy covering that organization.

OTIS, ROBERT, et al v GENERAL MOTORS CORP., et al
(Royal-Globe) (See also Sheppard v. General Motors)
Amount of Suit: Count I - $100,000.00; Count V - $100,000.00
Attorney: Gillespie, Burke and Gilespie (Patrick Cadagin)
File No.:   R-653A-16680 English
Cause No.:   69-L-809 Circuit Court Madison County
Summary: Date of Accident: 3/15/1968. Products Liability Case. 6:30 PM IL Route 121, 2 miles north of Harsburg, IL. Plaintiff's, traveling north in '68 Chevy when crossed centerline and collided head on with other automobile. Plaintiff's claim steering or brakes on auto were defective.

SHEPPARD, IZOLA, et al v GENERAL MOTORS CORPORATION, et al
(Royal-Globe) (See also Otis v General Motors)
Amount of Suit: $25,000.00 - $100,000.00
Attorney: Wiseman, Shaikewitz & McGivern
File No.:   R-653A-16680 English
Cause No.:   69-L-274 Circuit Court Madison County
Summary: Date of Accident: 3/15/1968. Products Liability Case. 6:30 PM IL Route 121, 2 miles north of Harsburg, IL. Plaintiff's, traveling south when Co-Defendant's, driving '68 Chevy north, crossed center line & collied with Plaintiffs. Plaintiff's claim steering or brakes on auto were defective.

FRENCH, GLENDA v SREDL, FREDERICK
(Royal-Globe)
Amount of Suit: $10,000.00
Attorney: Smith & Allen
File No.:   R-653A-23358 Langhammer
Cause No.:   72-M-454 Circuit Court Madison County
Summary: Date of Accident: 12/23/1971. 11:10 PM Route 157 at Holiday Inn entrance, Madison County. Defendant, south on 157 struck Plaintiff who entered Route 157 from Holiday Inn driveway.

TONER, CHARLES, JR. v THE FAIRFIELD ENGINEERING CO., et al
(Royal-Globe)
Amount of Suit: $50,000.00
Attorney: Smith, Allen, Moorman & Lakin
File No.:   OG 653A2982000 Temple
Cause No.:   USDC Alton
Summary: Date of Accident: 1/16/1972. Products Liability Case. Plaintiff's arm was amputated while using conveyer belt manufactured by Defendant.

JOHNSON, MICHELLE, et al v BOB'S FLOWER SHOP, INC., et al
(Northwestern National Insurance Group
Amount of Suit: Count I - $25,000.00; Count II - $10,000.00
Attorney: Kassly, Weihl and Bone, Becker & Carlson
File No.:   82-2331 - Gates
Cause No.:   75-L-1627
Summary: Date of Accident: 4/6/1974. 2:26 PM on Sherman Avenue, Belleville, IL. Defendant, traveling east in van, struck Plaintiff on bicycle.

EVANOFF, IRIS v BOWLAND, INC. (Royal-Globe)
Amount of Suit: $25,000.00
Attorney: Callis & Filcoff
File No.:   XP653A Wisdom
Cause No.:   74-L-654 Circuit Court Madison County
Summary: Date of Accident: 11/8/1972. 1:15 PM. Plaintiff fell on steps at Defendant's bowling alley.

MOLDED FIBER GLASS BODY CO. v GILMORE-OLSON CO., et al
(Continental Insurance Companies) (See Blackstone Mutual Insurance Co. v Gilmore-Olson.)
Amount of Suit: $82,829.99
Attorney: Hocker Godwin & MacGreevy/Murray & Stephens
File No.:   46 GLP 20284 Gerding
Cause No.:   66-141 Mariona County, Salem IL
Summary: Date of Accident: 12/8/1963. Assd. was general contractor constructing building for Plaintiff at Centralia, IL. Co-Defendant was Defendant's subcontractor actually doing the work. On 12/8/63 the building collapsed.

WALL, DARRELL v COUEY HARBOR SERVICE, aka C & S TOWING
(Joseph Kortenhof)
Amount of Suit: $50,000.00
Attorney: Pratt, Kardis & Strawn
File No.:   E 72-05629 Kortenhof
Cause No.:   74-L-115 Circuit Court Madison County
Summary: Date of Accident: 7/15/1972. Jones Act case. Plaintiff, a seamanor "ACE" was injured

BUSSMAN, ORVILLE H. Admr. v PENN CENTRAL, et al
Amount of Suit: $750,000.00
Attorney: Burroughs, Simpson & Wilson
File No.:   7.25076
Cause No.:   71-L-406 Circuit Court Madison County
Summary: Date of Accident: 4/24/1971. Wrongful death action. Grade crossing collision at 7th Street and Penn Central tracks in Charleston, IL at 11:40 PM.

S.S. KRESGE COMPANY v CLYDE J. HINES (Plaintiff Case)
Amount of Suit: Count I - $1,114.73; Count II - $1,114.73
Attorney: James W. McRoberts
File No.:   Gibson
Cause No.:   61-653 Circuit Court St. Clair County
Summary: Date of Accident: 4/29/1959. Defendant came into Plaintiff's premises at 211 Collinsville Avenue, E. St. Louis, IL to convert from heating to air conditioning and while doing so, caused damage to Plaintiff's property. A judgment has been entered against Defendant with the understanding that it will be collected against Defendant's insurance company only.

McGRAW, FOREST v GRANITE CITY STEEL v SERSTEL CORPORATION
(Underwriters)
Amount of Suit: $25,000.00
Attorney: Wm. Brandt
File No.:   046-4 B621 Gerding
Cause No.:   72-L-692 Circuit Court Madison County
Summary: Date of Accident: 12/22/1971. Wilson, general contractor for granite City Steel to repair furnaces. Serstel subcontractor for Wilson to do brick work. Plaintiff, an employee of Serstel, lost finger while opearing brick cutting saw. Plaintiff sues Wilson and Granite City Steel for negligence and Structural Work Act. Granite City Steel files third party complaint against Serstel for common law indemnity.

MAYBERRY, LEONARD W. v CIPS, et al
(Commercial Union)
Amount of Suit: $100,000.00
Attorney: Bill Schooley
File No.:   KF-5251 Wilde
Cause No.:   74-L-241 Circuit Court Madison County
Set for Trial: 11/18/1974
Summary: Date of Accident: 9/23/1971. CIPS plant in Coffeen, IL. Plaintiff, an employee of Daugherty Co., Inc. as pipefitter fell through grating.

PHILLIPS, VELMA, et al v AARON AMBULANCE SERVICE, et al
(Northwestern National)
Amount of Suit: $142,000.00
Attorney: John E. Norton
File No.: 29-5787 Brown
Cause No.: 73-L-3031 Circuit Court St. Clair County
Summary: Date of Accident: 9/22/1973. 8:20 PM at intersection of Eiler Road & Rt. 13. Plaintiff, west on Rt. 13, intending to make left turn onto Eiler Road. Defendant ambulance following Plaintiff and started to pass Plaintiff and struck Plaintiff as Plaintiff turned left.

WEBB, SILVANUS, SR., Administrator, etc. v NORFOLK AND WESTERN.
(See also Crews v N & W)
Amount of Suit: Three death cases
Attorney: Chapman, Talbert and Chapman
File No.: L-161-4612 Sample
Cause No.: 73-L-94 Madison County
Summary: Date of Accident: 7/2/1972. Three wrongful death cases. 3:10 PM 2 3/4 miles north of Litchfield. Grade crossing accident. Defendant's train south and Plaintiff's auto west on Varner Road.

CREWS, FRANCES v NORFOLK AND WESTERN RR.
(See also Webb v. N & W)
Amount of Suit: $500,000.00+
Attorney: William Schooley
File No.: L 125373 Sample
Cause No.: 72-L-519 Madison County
Summary: Date of Accident: 7/2/1972. Death and personal injury case. 3:10 PM 2¾ miles north of Litchfield. Grade crossing accident. Defendant's train south and Plaintiff's auto west on Varner Road

GREER, JANICE I., v KREMER, DR. OTTO L., et al
(Commercial Union)
Amount of Suit: $1,000,000.00
Attorney: Hotto and Adams (Neubauer)
File No.:   Wilde
Cause No.:   74-L-3092 Circuit Court St. Clair County
Summary: Date of Accident: 11/28/1973. Medical malpractice case. Plaintiff claims that Defendant performed myelogram on her without Plaintiff's consent.

REDNOUR, WILBURN L. v THE HERTZ CORPORATION, et al
(Royal-Globe)
Attorney: William Alexander
File No.:   XR653A25501 Temple
Cause No.:   74-CIV-13 Randolph County, Chester, IL
Summary: Date of Accident: 11/3/1973. Auto collision. 7:55 PM IL State Rt. 4, 3 miles south of Sparta, IL.

EMERSON, LORELEI v ALBERT JOLIVERT, MD, et al
(Commercial Union)
Amount of Suit: $750,000.00
Attorney: Sprague, Sprague and Ysursa
File No.:   K4-6923 Wilde
Cause No.:   73-L-1881 Circuit Court St. Clair County
Set for Trial: 12/2/1974
Summary: Date of Accident: 9/13-10/20/72. Patient of Dr. Jolivert admitted to St. Mary's Hospital re: chest pains. During treatment she was given certain blood-thinning drugs and in course of taking a blood sample her arm was injured, necessitating a subsequent operation.

PENNOCK, RUBY v GENERAL MOTORS CORPORATION, et al
(Royal-Globe)
Amount of Suit: $50,000.00
Attorney: Edward Neville
File No.:   R653A-23898 Heim
Cause No.:   71-2095 Circuit Court St. Clair County
Summary: Date of Accident: 4/7/1970. Product Liability case (1965 Pontiac Catalina). On Monsanto Avenue at S. 19th Street, St. Clair County, IL. Plaintiff, a passenger in an eastbound automobile on Monsanto was rear ended by Co-Defendant who was driving 1965 Pontiac. Plaintiff claims brakes on Pontiac were defective.

RANGE, ARTHUR, et al v IOWA PACKERS EXPRESS, INC. et al
(Empire Insurance Companies)
Attorney: Sprague, Sprague and Ysursa
File No.:   3-268175 Robert Kelley
Cause No.:   74-L-2628 Circuit Court St. Clair County
Summary: Date of Accident: 8/12/1973. 11:40 PM I-70, Saline County, MO. Co-Defendant entered I-70 to go westbound from EE and struck from rear by Defendant's westbound truck. Defendant crossed median and hit Plaintiff's eastbound motor home.

ROSENKRANZ, RAY E. v GENERAL MOTORS CORPORATION, et al
(Royal-Globe)
Amount of Suit: $60,000.00
Attorney: Robert E. McGlynn
File No.:   1R653A27736 Temple
Cause No.:   73-L-2955 Circuit Court St. Clair County
Summary: Date of Accident: 9/11/1972. 1:00 PM at Defendant's plant at 3809 Union Blvd., St. Louis, MO. Plaintiff, a switchman for Terminal, injured when he stepped on a tie which had greaese on it. FELA action against railroad and negligence action against GM.

PAYER, JOHN L. v GENERAL MOTORS
(Royal-Globe)
Amount of Suit: $35,000.00
Attorney: McGlynn and McGlynn
File No.:   R654A-21483 English
Cause No.:   73-L-1182 Circuit Court St. Clair County
Summary: Date of Accident: 4/24/1971. 9:00 PM at GM Assembly Plant in St. Louis, MO. Plaintiff, walking on loading dock adjacent to Track 4 caught right foot in hole on dock. Sprained right knee.

FIRST GRANITE CITY NATIONAL BANK, Admr. of the Estate of Robert McLarnan v GENERAL MOTORS CORP (Royal-Globe)
Amount of Suit: $350,000.00
Attorney: Chapman and Chapman
File No.:   PL10471 Enderby
Cause No.:   76-L-484 Circuit Court Madison County
Summary: Date of Accident: 7/6/1974. Wrongful death case; Products Liability case involving 1973 Chevrolet Blazer. Tuetken Corner in Jerey County, IL.

MAKROVITCH CARROLL T., et al v GENERAL MOTORS CORP., et al
Amount of Suit: $15,000.00
Attorney: David Wahl
Cause No.:   76-L-687 Circuit Court Madison County
Summary: Date of Accident: 5/5/1976. 12:20 PM Co-Defendant Phipps, operating a 1970 Pontiac Grand Prix in northerly direction on IL Rt. 3 in E. Alton, struck auto driven by Co-Defendant Ebbler. Ebbler struck a parked pickup truck in which Plaintiff was sitting. Plaintiffs allege right front tie rod and tie rod adjusting sleeve broke causing the Pontiac to veer out of control and strike car driven by Ebbler.

NATIONAL OATS COMPANY v VOLKMAN, ADOLPH
(Hartford)
File No.: 46 L 7181 Heid
Summary: Date of Accident: 1/10/1965. Indemnity action arising out of accident which occurred at 3:30 PM resulting in the death of Carl H. Volkman when he was killed riding a manlift on Plaintiff's premises.

CHARLENE HUNTER v DONALD INGRAM & SQUIBB
Amount of Suit: $3,000.00
Attorney: Burroughs, Simpson & Wilson
File No.: Employers K4-6702
Cause No.: 72-L-593
Summary: Date of Accident: August/September 1972. Plaintiff, being treated for hayfever. Kenelog 40 injected in to arm. Atrophy of fatty tissue – should have been injected into butt.

GERMANIA FEDERAL SAVINGS AND LOAN ASSN. v UNITED GUARANTEE RESIDENTIAL INSURANCE CO. of IOWA
Amount of Suit: $1,475,988.74
Attorney: Bob Maucker
File No.: John L. Rendleman, Greensboro, NC
Cause No.: A-CIV-750050 USDC, Southern Division
Summary: Suit on loan insurance.

FRONTIER INVESTMENT CORP. v FUSZ-SCHMELZLE & CO., INC. et al (Lewis, Rice, Tucker, Alen andChubb) (See also Joiner, et al v Fusz-Schmelzle)
Amount of Suit: Injunction Suit
Attorney: Meyer and Meyer
File No.: MA-11731
Cause No.: 66-4001 & 67-7149 Circuit Court St. Clair County
Summary: We are local counsel

BRUEGGEMAN, MICHAEL v HERSEL LILLIS, JR.
Amount of Suit: $75,000.00
Cause No.: Circuit Court St. Clair County
Summary: Date of Accident: 9/23/1973. 12:39 AM in 1800 block of South Belt West, Belleville, IL. Plaintiff, traveling west and Defendant, traveling east. Defendant swerved on the wrong side of highway and sideswiped Plaintiff.

GUSHLEFF v SEEBOLD (two minors)
Amount of Suit: Count I - $50,000.00, Count II - $15,000.00
Attorney: Callis
File No.: C653A25709
Cause No.: 73-L-228 Ed
Summary: Date of Accident: 12/21/1972. Plaintiff, south of Madison in Granite City near 16th Street. Defendant out from Granite City Steel enters southbound lane.

SCROGGINS v BURKE BROS.
Amount of Suit: Count I - $50,000; Count II - $25,000
Attorney: T. Francis
File No.: K4-5792
Cause No.: 73-L-389 Ed
Summary: Date of Accident: 10/5/1972. Defendant rear ended Plaintiff at Pontoon Rd & Mameski.

DOWLAND, RONALD v TURPIN, GARY
Amount of Suit: $100,000.00
Attorney: Kinder
File No.: K4-5608
Cause No.: 73-32 7th Circuit Court Green County
Summary: Date of Accident: 8/10/1971. Plaintiff hit horse in motorcycle accident. FX arm reduced by Defendant. Reduction slipped.

SCHARF v PLANT v BOWEN & FLEETWOOD CHEVY
Amount of Suit: Count I - $9,500.00; Count II - $9,500.00
Attorney: Hamilton
File No.: Royal R 653A25786
Cause No.: Bell 73-I-2341
Summary: Date of Accident: 12/24/1971. Rt. 460 near Freeburg. Both Plaintiff and Defendant on Rt. 460. Defendant tried to pass seveeral cars and Plaintiff turned left in front of him.

JORDON, SHIRLEY v DONALD HALL
Amount of Suit: $100,000.00
Attorney: Williamson
File No.: Royal R653A27002
Cause No.: 73-L-647
Summary: Date of Accident: 6/24/1973. Easton & Broadway, Alton, IL. Defendant rear ended Plaintiff.

NORTH v MANOR BAKING CO. (See Alfaro v Manor
Amount of Suit: Count I - $100,000.00; Count II - $25,000.00;
Count III - $10,000.00
Attorney: P - Schooley; Firestone - Talbert;
Sayre & Fisher - Ducey
File No.: Royal R653A24719
Cause No.: 72-L-536 USDC
Summary: Date of Accident: 8/12/1972. Defendant's semi blew right front tire, went off 220 into trailer park killing little girl.

RADIC v STEPHENS d/b/a TRI CO
Amount of Suit: $15,500.00
Attorney: O'Donnell
File No.: Employers K4-4545
Cause No.: 72-1518
Summary: Date of Accident: Oct-71. Building blew over.

PETER LECCE v CHAMPION FINANCE
Amount of Suit: $9,000.00
Attorney: Kaucher
File No.: Commercial K4-7158
Cause No.: 74-122
Summary: Staunton Rt. 66. Defendant, going east turning left to go North. Plaintiff going south

TURLEY v BIEDERMANS & AUTOCRAT
Amount of Suit: $80,000.00
Attorney: John Bosh
File No.:   Employers K4-3619
Cause No.:   Belleville 71-1215
Summary: Date of Accident: 7/2/1969. Plaintifff deceased from electric shock from stove manufactured by Autocrat and sold by Biedermans.

AALCO SUPPLY v HARVEY ALUMINUM
(Commercial Union)
Amount of Suit: $2,370.48
Attorney: Chas. Kolker
File No.:   Wilde
Cause No.:   72-2768 Circuit Court St. Clair County
Summary: Defendant sold bad fittings. Defendant has never been served.

GALATI, KATHRYN v TISCHKAU, J, et al
Cause No.:   74-19 Circuit Court Ft. Myers FL
Summary: Date of Accident: 6/11/1972. Plaintiff, a passenger in southbound car drive by Defendant. Barr on Rt. 867, Ft. Myers, FL, when it hit concrete wall.

RUPPEL, FRED Admr v B&O and GENERAL MOTORS CORPORATION
Attorney: Callis and Hartman
Cause No.: 78-L- 89 Circuit Court Madison County
Summary: We are local counsel

KENNETH, Admr., v GENERAL MOTORS CORP., and VERNON SMALL CHEVROLET-OLDS, INC. (Royal Globe) (See also Suydam v GM)
Amount of Suit: Excess of $15,000.00
Attorney: Norton, Bonifield & Associates
File No.: Ray Shultz
Cause No.: 79-L-928 Circuit Court St. Clair County
Summary: Date of Accident: 5/24/1979. 7:04 PM on Hwy. 50 in O'Fallon, IL. Plaintiff decedant was driving his Vega in an easterly direction on Rt. 50 when left rear wheel became detached from the auto causing the auto to crash into an approaching auto.

DURBIN, DANIEL J. v GENERAL MOTORS CORPORATION, et al (Royal Globe)
Amount of Suit: Excess of $15,000.00
Attorney: Bruce Cook
Cause No.: 82-L-186 Circuit Court St. Clair County
Summary: Date of Accident: 4/24/1981. Product Liability case involving 1977 Chevy truck at Renault, IL. Plaintiff, standing beside truck when radiator exploded causing scalding water to strike Plaintiff.

AULT, JOHN ROBERT v GENERAL MOTORS CORPORATION, et al (Royal-Globe)
Amount of Suit: Excess of $15,000.00
Attorney: Wm. W. Schooley
Cause No.:   82-L-97 Circuit Court Madison County
Summary: Date of Accident: 12/8/1978. Product Liability case involving 1978 Chevy pickup on Hwy. 51, 3 miles north of Sandoval, IL. Plaintiff, driving north on 51 when truck went out of control and rolled over. Plaintiff claims that accident was due to a defective tie-rod.

NEUWIRTH, RICHARD v GENERAL MOTORS CORPORATION (Royal-Globe)
Amount of Suit: Excess of $15,000.00
Attorney: Rick Rosen
Cause No.:   82-L-850 Circuit Court St. Clair County
Summary: Date of Accident: 10/12/1980. Plaintiff claims while Chevy Nova was being driven by James G. Prather in an easterly direction on IL Rt. 15 near Freeburg Care Center in Freeburg, IL, the auto struck a curb and overturned fracturing the rear axle and causing the right wheel to come off.

JORDAN, ROY v CORMAC, INC. and ISOWA INDUSTRY CO. LTD.
Amount of Suit: Excess of $15,000.00
Attorney: Donald S. Singer
File No.:   15-404588 J. McConnell
Cause No.:   84-5344 USDC Alton, IL
Summary: Date of Accident: 8/24/1982. Products Liability case involving printer-slotter machine Model PS7. Plaintiff was unjamming machine when he was injured. Defendant manufactured the machine

CITY NATIONAL BANK & TRUST CO. (Estate of Jennifer Chapman) v
GENERAL MOTORS CORPORATION (See also Pipple, Margaret L. v GM)
Amount of Suit: Excess of $15,000.00
Attorney: C.E. Heiligenstein
Cause No.:   83-L-357 Circuit Court St. Clair County
Summary: Date of Accident: 6/13/1981. Involving a 1975 Chevy Scottsdale truck at the intersection of east-west Windsor Road and north-south North 2nd Street in Winnebago County, IL. Plaintiff, a minor, was riding as a passenger in the Chevy truck that was being driven in an easterly direction on Windsor Road by Margaret Pipple. Clark D. Schoon was driving an ambulance for Co-Defendant in a northerly direction on North 2nd Street. The vehicles collided at the intersection. The Chevy truck burst into flames. Plaintiff claims that the truck had a defective fuel containing system.

PIPPLE, MARGARET L. v GENERL MOTORS CORPORATION
(See also City National Bank & Trust v GM)
Amount of Suit: Excess of $15,000.00
Attorney: Jerald J. Bonifield
Cause No.:   83-L-492 Circuit Court St. Clair County
Summary: Date of Accident: 6/13/1981. Intersection of east-west Windsor Road and north-south 2nd Street in Winnebago County, IL. Plaintiff was drving a 1975 Chevy Scottsdale truck in an easterly directoin on Windsor Road. Clark D. Schoon was driving an ambulance for Co-Defendant in a northerly direction on North 2nd Street. The vehicles collided at the intersection. The Chevy truck burst into flames. Plaintiff claims that the Chevy truck had a defective fuel containing system.

FAYETTE FARMERS v LARRY LeFEVRE and ZEMAN & OLDFIELD LAW GROUP LTD. (Cincinnati Insurance Co.)
Attorney: Thompson & Mitchell - Robert Brownlee
Cause No.:   83-5084 USDC Souther District
Summary: Defendant's are being sued on basis of respondant superior. Suit arise out of a joint venture involving farm land which was put together by Crawford who is now deceased.

PIPES, ROBERT W., et al v JOHN ENTWISTLE, JERRY NELSON, d/b/a Nelson Construction Co. & American Logging (Royal-Globe)
Amount of Suit: Excess of $15,000.00
Attorney: Ronald L. Carpel
File No.:   691 A 18805 Koehler
Cause No.:   81-L-1090 Circuit Court St. Clair County
Summary: Date of Accident: 3/28/1980. 9:15 AM at the premises of Clyde Dial Construction Co., in Decatur, IL. Dial sold a used 8 x 20 foot gas storage tank to Jerry Nelson. Nelson and his employee, John Entwistle, intended to remove the tank with Nelson's flatbed lowboy trailer. Jim Hutchcraft, an employee of Dial, loaded the tank onto thelowboy with a crane. Nelson and Entwistle proceeded to secure the tank with chains. While they were in the process of tightening down the tank at the rear with a chain tightener, Pipes, an office employee of Dial, approached the operation to assist Nelson and Entwistle. As Plaintiff got close to Entwistle and Nelson, the pipe being used by them to tighten the handle sliped and struck Plaintiff in the face.

FRIEDERICH, DONNA v KIMBERLY CLARK
Attorney: Heiligenstein
Cause No.:   u1-L-166 Circuit Court St. Clair County
Summary: Products Liability case invovling Kotex manufactured by Kimberly Clark. Plaintiff claims that she sustained "toxic shock sydrome" as the result of using Kotex tampons.

BEAVERS, CHARLES D. v MONTGOMERY ELEVATOR CO., et al
Amount of Suit: Excess of $15,000.00
Attorney: Con, Carr, Korein, Kunin, Schlichter & Brennan –
                    Rick Jones
Cause No.:   8a-L-1225 Circuit Court Madison County
Set for Trial: 11/12/1985
Summary: Negligence and Scaffold Act case at Illinois Elderly Housing in Mt. Vernon, IL. Defendant, a subcontractor installing elevators, is being sued by Plaintiff, an employee of painting subcontractor who fell through open elevator shaft.

ZEZOFF, DAVID L. v ARCHER DANIELS MIDLAND CORP
(Crawford & Co.)
Amount of Suit: Excess of $15,000.00
Attorney: Gitchoff & Wallis
File No.:   261-13953 SE Steve Edmunds
Cause No.:   81-L-604 Circuit Court Madison County
Summary: Date of Accident: 3/20/1980. Archer Daniels, owner of property, contracted with Federal Steel & Supply Co. to construct a structure on the premises. Plaintiff, an employee of Federal Steel fell from a scaffold.

BRADLEY, JACK v GENERAL MOTORS
Attorney: Tietz & Heavner
Cause No.:   81-L-449 Circuit Court Madison County
Summary: Date of Accident: 4/24/1979. 2:00 AM in 1000 block of E. West, E. Eldorado St., Decatur, IL. Plaintiff, operating a 1977 Buick Special which was stopped on E. Eldorado Street facing in easterly direction when rear ended by a 1972 Chevy Nova being driven by James Harmon. The fuel tank of Buick punctured as the result of the collision and the Buick became engulfed in flame.

LAUX, BONNIE & JOHN v GENERAL MOTORS CORPORATION
(Royal-Globe)
Amount of Suit: Excess of $15,000.00
Attorney: Kaucher, Collins & Ligman - Douglas Hamman
Cause No.:   81-L-716 Circuit Court Madison County
Summary: Date of Accident: 7/12/1979. Round Table Restaurant parking lot in Collinsville, IL. Plaintiff's claim a Delco battery which was installed in their 1977 Chevy Malibu exploded and injured Bonnie Laux and damaged their auto.

HAYES, MURIEL v THE BAYER COMPANY, GLENBROOK LABORATORIES
DIVISION of STERLING DRUGS, Inc. (Royal-Globe)
Amount of Suit: $100,000.00 actual; $10,000,000.00 punitive
Attorney: Shaikewitz, McGivern & Wahl
File No.: RG 653A-60670
Cause No.: 881-5015 USDC Southern District
Summary: Date of Accident: 9/13/1980. Plaintiff claims she started taking aspirin (Bayer Timed-Release) for a sore throat in early September 1980. Aspirin purchased at Wal-Mart in Jerseyville, IL. Plaintiff took 2 at night and 2 in the morning. On September 13, 1980, while visitng friends in Salem, Oregon, Plaintiff fainted and was taken to Salem Memorial Hospital where she was suffering from upper gastrointestinal bleeding probably aspirin induced.

ZIMMERMAN, ZITA v GLENNON TRANSPORTATION
(Commercial Union)
Amount of Suit: Excess of $15,000.00
Attorney: Robert Larson
File No.: Tom Held
Cause No.: 81-L-907
Summary: Date of Accident: 6/1/1981. 7:30 AM Rt. 111 at 35 in Madison County, IL. Plaintiff's southbound car stopped for red light at Rt. 35 when it was rear ended by Defendant's southbound tractor-trailer truck

WILSON'S DOOR CO., INC. v GLENN WEEKS, INC. d/b/a Glenn Weeks
Pontiac-Chevrolet
Amount of Suit: Excess of $10,000.00
Attorney: Campbell, Furnall, Moore & Jacobson –
Jerome McDonald
Cause No.: u8a-L-55 Circuit Court Jefferson County
Set for Trial: 1/26/1980
Summary: Plaintiff purchased a new 1980 Chevy 1-ton truck from Defendant. Plaintiff's suit is based upon breach of implied warranty of merchantability, breach of implied warranty of fitness, breach of express warranty and inadequate repairs.

JAECKEL, ROBERT v GRUMLEY FORD-MERCURY, INC., & DICK HAUSER d/b/a DICK HAUSER MOTORS - DICK HAUSER v DAIRYLAND INSURANCE CO. & BE SHARM (Sentry Insurance)
Amount of Suit: $25,000.00
Attorney: Pessin, Baird & Wells
File No.: CL 25-52734 Darrell Zabrocki
Cause No.: 81-L-163 Circuit Court St. Clair County
Summary: Defense on behalf of third part, Dairyland Insurance Co. Insured, Ben Sharm, reported that his 1979 Chevy Chevette had been stolen. It was not but Sharm sold the auto to Dick Hauser who sold the vehicle to Grumley Ford-Mercury, who sold the car to Plaintiff Robert Jaeckel. When Dairyland located the vehicle, they secured a duplicate title from their insured, took the auto from Illinois to Nebraska. Plaintiff is suing Grumley Ford-Mercury and Dick Hauser and Dick Hauser is suing Dairyland Insurance Co.

WALIGORSKI, KENNETH, father and next friend of KRISTOPHER MICHAEL WALKGORSKI, a minor v HEWLETT-PACKARD MFG. CO, WINTHROP LABS, INC., A.H. ROBBINS CORP., OLIVER ANDERSON HOSPITAL, Dr. PETER BARTSCH, DR. ROBERT GRAVES and DR. ANITA BASA
Amount of Suit: Excess of $15,000.00
Attorney: P - Amiel Queto;
Winthrop - Garrheson & Santori - Frank McAleenan
File No.: O-S-636-A-88919 Pat Martin
Cause No.: 81-L-880 Circuit Court St. Clair County
Summary: Date of Accident: 1/27/1981. Plaintiff's son born on 1/27/81. Plaintiff's mother had taken Demoral manufactured by Winthrop Lab. Plaintiff claims this resulted in his osn being paralyzed and suffering from brain damage.

CHURCHMAN v NISSAN
Amount of Suit: Excess of $15,000.00
Attorney: Bruce Cook
Cause No.: 82-L-210 Circuit Court St. Clair County
Set for Trial: 4/8/1986
Summary: Date of Accident: 10/14/1981. Products Liability case involving 1980 Datsun. Minor Plaintiff, standing in front of Datsun claims shift lever slipped from park to drive causing auto to strike Plaintiff

GOEHRING, AUGUST W. v A.E. STALEY MFG. CO. v BODINE ELECTRIC (Commercial Union)
Amount of Suit: Excess of $15,000.00
Attorney: P: Wm. Schooley; Staley - Larry Hepler
File No.: Darlene Logue
Cause No.: 83-L-14 Circuit Court Madison County
Summary: Date of Accident: 5/5/1982. 11:00 AM, Building 29, Staley Mfg. Co., Decatur, IL. Plaintiff, an electrician employed by Bodine, stepped back into open trench and fell.

ROWLAND, JACK v DUNLOP TIRE & RUBBER CORPORATION & PETER BALDINO (Royal-Globe)
Amount of Suit: $750,000.00
Attorney: Norton, Bonifield & Associates
File No.: 653A-69203 Kettwich
Cause No.: 82-L-517 Circuit Court St. Clair County
Summary: Date of Accident: 5/13/1982. 8:00 AM on IL State Rt. 149 in Franklin County, IL. Plaintiff, driving 1972 Oldsmobile in easterly direction. Plaintiff claims left front tire on Baldino's van (a Dunlop tire) blew out causing the van to cross the center line and collide head-on with Plaintiff's auto.

DECKER, TONI L., Special Admr., estate of Richard Decker v WINTHROP LABORATORIES, INC., et al (Royal-Globe)
Amount of Suit: Excess of $15,000.00
Attorney: Amiel Cueto
File No.: 653A76357 Watts
Cause No.: 83-L-1082 Circuit Court St. Clair County
Summary: Date of Accident: 12/30/1981. Products Liability & Wrongful Death case. Plaintiff claims that deceased died following a brain aneurysm resulting from the intake of Demoral manufactued by Winthrop.

DILLMAN, EDWARD, et al v MEMCO, DECO, OLD BEN COAL CO., & LUCAS GIRLING, LTD.
Amount of Suit: $100,000.00
Attorney: P - Robert C. Nelson; Memco - John McMulin; DECO - Jos. Davidson
File No.: LO-1242 Jim Hubbard
Cause No.: USDA Alton, IL
Summary: Date of Accident: 2/9/1983. Plaintiff, operating a golf cart in Old Ben Coal Co. mine, when something about the golf cart malfunctioned resulting in an accident. Dillman is a quadriplegic or paraplegic.

VITTITOW, JOSEPH v SHELL OIL COMPANY, et al , McCartin, McAuliffe Mechanical Contractors - 3rd Party Plaintiff v Modern Electric Co., 3rd Party Defendant (Commerical Union)
Attorney: P - Steve Tillery; Shell - Shephard, Sandberg, etc.; McCartin, McAuliff - Almeter
Cause No.: 81-L-1160 Circuit Court Madison County
Summary: Date of Accident: 11/16/1979. Shell Oil storage facility in Patoka, IL. Plaintiff, an employee of Modern Electric working as a borrowed employee of McCartin-McAuliffe to install fire alarm system. Plaintiff, working on storage tank #710 when crude oil inadvertently pumped into tank.

STEMMLER, ALFRED, Special Admr. Of the estate of DEBORAH STEMMLER, deceased v PRIDE SERVICES, INC., PROFESSIONAL X-RAY, INC., RICHARD HACKER, and VOLKSWAGEN OF AMERICA
Amount of Suit: Excess of $15,000.00
Attorney: Thomas Q. Keefe, Jr.
File No.: 24R01812/71
Cause No.: 83-L-49 Circuit Court St. Clair County
Summary: Date of Accident: 7/28/1982. Prodcuts Liability case involving a 1972 Type I (Beetle or Super Beetle). Accident at I-55 in Grundy County, IL. Deceased's VW collided with rear of GMC Sierra truck which was parked on the shoulder of the road. The VW erupted into fire and Plaintiff's decedent died as a result.

TITTER, VIOLA, Admr. V THE UPJOHN COMPANY, et al
Amount of Suit: Excess of $15,000.00
Attorney: Amiel Cueto
Cause No.: 83-L-571 Circuit Court St. Clair County
Summary: Date of Accident: 9/29/1982. Product Liability case involving Upjohn's product - Motrin.

HENRY, ERICA, a minor by Thomas Henry, her father and next friend v BREON LABORATORIES, et al (Royal-Globe)
Amount of Suit: Excess of $15,000.00
Attorney: Bruce Cook
File No.: 8s 691 A 23604 - Fred F. Koehler
Cause No.: 83-L-295 Circuit Court Sangamon County
Summary: Date of Accident: 8/17/1982. Products Liability case involving Marcaine, an anesthetic. Plaintiff's mother was given Marcaine during delivery of Plaintiff at St. John's Hospital in Springfield, IL. The Marcaine was administered by a paracervical block. This is not recommended. Plaintiff now has brain damage.

HAYTER, BRUCE and DEBORAH v KERO-SUN, Inc., STERLING DISTRIBUTING CO., INC., ALTON STONE & FIREPLACE CENTER, INC., and TOYOTOMI KOGYO CO., LTD. (Tokio Marine & Fire Insurance Co. Ltd. of Japan)
Amount of Suit: Excess of $15,000.00
Attorney: Levy & Levy
File No.: 6LL84-4463-T Daniel F. Tront
Cause No.: 83-L-929 Circuit Court Madison County
Summary: Date of Accident: 2/2/1982. Plaintiff's claim that they purchased a Kero-Sun heather from Alton Stone & Fireplace Center. Plaintiff's claim that the heater emitted excessive levels of kerosene vapor and smoke resulting in damage to Plalintiff's.

BECKER, BARBRA, Special Admr. of the estate of Danny Becker, deceased v THE UPJOHN COMPANY, et al
Amount of Suit: Excess of $15,000.00
Attorney: Bruce Cook
File No.: 11647 Bill Bush
Cause No.: 83-L-374 Circuit Court St. Clair County
Set for Trial: Pending
Summary: Date of Accident: 3/5/1983. Plaintiff's decedent took a Medrol tablet which caused him to hallucinate and become disoriented and depressed so that he committed suicide.

EDEN, RICHARD v CONTINENTAL CAN COMPANY
Amount of Suit: Excess of $15,000.00
Attorney: Amiel Cueto
File No.: John Garrigan - Continental Can
Cause No.: 83-L-1081 Circuit Court St. Clair County
Summary: Date of Accident: 6/9/1983. Product Liability case involving can of Penetrating Oil. Plaintiff used blow torch near penetrating oil when can exploded.

CEDRIC CLARKSON v ST. CLAIR SQUARE, INC.; PRIMAC CENTER ASSOCIATION, LP & MAY CENTER, INC. v MONTGOMERY ELEVATOR EXPORT CORP.
Amount of Suit: Excess of $15,000.00
Attorney: P - James P. Stiehl; Co-D - Joseph Hickey
Cause No.:   83-L-896
Set for Trial: 12/10/1985
Summary: Date of Accident: 10/18/1981. St. Clair Square, Fairview Heights. Plaintiff claims he was injured while riding an escalator.

KINTSTLER, JERRY DEAN v JOY MANUFACTURING
Amount of Suit: Excess of $15,000.00
Attorney: Robert Nelson
File No.:   11-12-077 Dennis Morgenstern
Cause No.:   83-L-730 Circuit Court St. Clair County
Set for Trial: 10/16/1989
Summary: Date of Accident: 12/11/1981. Product Liability Case. Accident occurred at River King Mine of Peabody Coal Co. in Freeburgh, IL. Plaintiff was operating the shuttle car, moving the machine backwards. In backing up he backed underneath a parked machine and caught his right foot between the bumper of the other machine and where his foot was on the frame of his machine. His right foot was crushed.

MID-AMERICA BANK & TRUST COMPANY (STREUMPF) v JAMES K. ALMETER (WTC) (See also Klenke v Almeter)
Amount of Suit: $686,536.50
Attorney: Jerry Bonifield
File No.:   01-2847-624-9818 Wesley Steuber
Cause No.:   84-L-776 Circuit Court Madison County
Summary: Almeter was employed by Commerical Union to represent Wilmer Klenke. The coverage was $50,000.00. Plaintiff offered to settle for maximum insurance coverage and Commerical Union authorized Almeter to settle for that amount. Almeter offered $30,000.00 and thereafter there was an excess verdict. The insured assigned his cause of action to the Plaintiff so that this suit is brought against Commerical Union and Almeter for negligence.

KLENKE, WILMER v JAMES K. ALAMETER
(National Union Fire Insurance Co.) (See also Mid-America Bank v Almeter)
Amount of Suit: $861.536.50
Attorney: Burton C. Bernard
File No.:   01-2847-6249818 Wesley Steuber
Cause No.:   84-L-105 Circuit Court Madison County
Summary: Almeter was employed by Commerical Union to represent Wilmer Klenke. Commercial coverage was $50,000.00. Plaintiff offered to settle for maximum insurance coverage and Commerical Union authorized Almeter to settle for that amount. Almeter, rather than offfering the maximum amount of his authority, advised Plaintiff's attorney that he had authority to settle for $30,000.00 . Thereafter, Plaintiff's attorney withdrew his offer to settle for $50,000.00 and now refuses to settle within the policy limits. Shortly thereafter, Almeter offered the $50,000.00 limit but Plaintiff refused to accept the offer.

SCHNEIDEWIND, DONNA v MONTGOMERY ELEVATOR
Amount of Suit: Under $15,000.00
Attorney: Dakin Williams
File No.:   Karen Scopel, Commercial Union
Cause No.:   83-Lm-2073 Circuit Court St. Clair County
Set for Trial: 4/786
Summary: Date of Accident: 11/2/1981. Product Liability case involving down escalator at St. Clair Square Mall. Plaintiff's right shoe became stuck in escalator causing Plaintiff to twist right ankle.

BUSHART, STEVE & DARLENE v RALPH SCHANZ & BERNETTE SCHANZ & 3rd PARTY PLAINTIFFS v PEABODY COAL & JACK BYRD
Amount of Suit: $72,000.00
Attorney: Kuehn & Rhein
Cause No.:   84-L-619 Circuit Court St. Clair County
Summary: Subsidence Case

SEIFERT, CHARLENE, a minor, etc. v. THE UPJOHN COMPANY (Aetna)
Attorney: Jerome Mirza
File No.: Harold J. Decker
Cause No.: 84-520 USDC Alton
Set for Trial: 4/7/1976
Summary: Plaintiff claims mother was given Provera to prevent habitual abortion. Plaintiff claims that as a result of this drug she has a birth defect.

LEE, PAUL v TEREX CORP, & EBBLER & GM
Attorney: P - Tom Keefe, Jr; Ebbler - Dennis Rose
Cause No.: 86-L-995 Circuit Court St. Clair County
Set for Trial: 5/29/1990
Summary: Date of Accident: 4/4/1985. Plaintiff, driving an 85-ton Terex truck which had been repaired by Co-Defendant Ebbler. Ebbler manufactures hoses and clamps. As Plaintiff was operating truck, a hose or clamp came loose, squirted diesel fuel across engine which resulted in a fire. Plaintiff severely burned.

JAMES, RICHARD v WINTHROP LABORATORIES, et al (Royal)
Amount of Suit: Excess of $15,000.00
Attorney: P - Amiel Cueto; Royal - D.M. Kirk
File No.: 653A-81774 Ken Boland
Cause No.: 85-L-121 Circuit Court St. Clair County
Summary: Date of Accident: 4/26/1982. Product Liability case involving Demerol. Plaintiff claims he was brain damaged at birth as the result of Demerol.

KOPITSKY, HARVEY v VWOA, VW MID-AMERICA
Amount of Suit: $5,000.00; Punitiive - $250,000.00
Attorney: Tom Halverson
File No.: 22S02924/84 Bill Guida
Cause No.: 852-0055-Division 1 Circuit Court City of St. Louis
Summary: Date of Accident: 3/15/1984. Product Liability case involving 1984 Audi 5000. Audi allegedly accerlated and collided with building. Vehicle was subject to recall campaign.

BROOKS, DENNIS v S.C. JOHNSON & SON, INC.
Amount of Suit: Exceeds $10,000.00
Attorney: Gerald L. Montroy
File No.: 10694/94785 Gary Van Domelen
Cause No.: CV 86-4136 USDC-Southern District-Benton
Set for Trial: 9/11/1989
Summary: Date of Accident: 8/10/1985. Product Liability case involving Raid Flea Killer. Plaintiff sprayed his room with flea killer, went to bed and later was partially paralyzed.

DENNIS L. SNELL v LAURA BUICK-PONTIAC-GM INC v PONTIAC DIVISION OF GM CORPORATION
Amount of Suit: Contribution
Attorney: P - Steven D. Grimm;
Laura Buick - Brian K. McBrearty
Cause No.: 87-L-327 Circuit Court Madison County
Set for Trial: 11/18/1991
Summary: Date of Accident: 9/20/1987. Main Street in Glen Carbon, Madison County, IL. Product Liability case involving a 1986 Pontiac Grand Am. Plaintiff was operating Gran Am in a westerly direction on Main Street when the engine stalled. Plaintiff alleges that this caused him to collide with a parked automobile.

SINK, JULIA & LAURA v AUDI OF AMERICA
Amount of Suit: $100,000.00
Attorney: Daniel R. Devereaux
File No.:   Guida File 23W04124/85
Cause No.:   87-0513-C-2 USDC Easter District of MO
Summary: Date of Accident: 2/15/1986 & 3/7/9186. Product Liability case involving a 1985 Audi. Plaintiff claims that she leased this vehilce on June 26, 1985 from Plaza Motor. Plaintiff claims the vehicle was defective at the time she leased it because the brakes unexpectedly locked on repeated occassions. Her suit is based upon many theories, including fraud, product liability, etc., and she wants to be released from the terms of her lease.

TAFT, DARRELL & JOHN HOOD v JOY MANUFACTURING CO.
Attorney: Joe Bartholomew
Cause No.:   87-5240 Beatty
Set for Trial: May-88
Summary: Date of Accident: 8/31/1985 - Taft; 2/14/1986 - Hood. Plaintiffs, employees of Peabody Coal at Baldwin Mine #1, injured when pan of the continuous miner dropped while Plaintiff attempting to pump oil into continuous miner.

FAUKE, MARY LOU v JOY MANUFACTURING CO.
Amount of Suit: Excess of $15,000.00
Attorney: Tom Keefe
Cause No.:   87-4388 USDC Souther District Benton
Set for Trial: 1/9/1998
Summary: Date of Accident: 2/25/1985. Product Liability case involving a shuttle car manufactured by Joy. Plaintiff, operating Joy Shuttle Car at Monterey Coal Mine when it struck a hole resulting in injuries to her back, etc. (Ruptered disc).

BROOKS, JACKIE v MONTGOMERY ELEVATOR CO., et al
Amount of Suit: Excess of $15,000.00
Attorney: Christopher Cueto
File No.:   P441-12696-01
Cause No.:   88-L-471 Circuit Court St. Clair County
Summary: Date of Accident: 11/28/1987. St. Clair Square, Fairview Heights, IL. Plaintiff riding "UP" escalator when she claims it suddenly stopped causing her to lose her balance and fall down the escaltor.

CALVERT, EVERETT v TOYOTOMI AMERICA, INC., KERO-SUN, INC., & K.S. WHOLESELLERS OF AMERICA, INC. (Tokio Marine & Fire Insurance Co.)
Amount of Suit: $2,500,000.00
Attorney: Eric S. Pistorius
File No.:   6LL89-0014-T
Cause No.:   88-3816
Summary: Date of Accident: 12/24/1986. Kerosene heater caught fire. Plaintiff suffered personal injuries, also property damage.

ENGLAND, GARY v JOY MANUFACTURING & AMERICAN MINING CONGRES
Amount of Suit: Excess of $15,000.00
Attorney: Tom Keefe
File No.:   11-12-162
Cause No.:   USDC 88-4098 - Benton
Set for Trial: 4/20/1992
Summary: Date of Accident: 12/12/1986. Plaintiff, employed by Consolidated Coal in McLeansboro, IL, operator of a shuttle car, ran into a hole or other obstruction in the travelway of mine that caused him to be bounced rom the seat of the vehicle.

DELVECCHIO, FRANK, etc. v. GENERAL MOTORS CORP. & B.B.B. MOTOR CO., INC.
Amount of Suit: Excess of $15,000.00
Attorney: Amiel Cueto
File No.: GM 110465 Silverman
Cause No.: 89-L-66 Circuit Court St. Clair County
Set for Trial: 12/17/1990
Summary: Date of Accident: 12/10/1988. Plaintiff, driving 1987 Olds Cutlass Brougham International, at the intersection of 159 and Rt. 15. As he was approaching a stopped line of traffic, the warning light flashed on the automobile and Plaintiff claims he had no brakes or steering. He was able to swerve the auto to the left resulting in a collision with a ditch. Plaintiff's wife was killed and he was severely injured.

LITTLE, JACQUELINE v GENERAL MOTORS CORP., et al
Amount of Suit: Excess of $15,000.00
Attorney: Gregory A Becker
File No.: 123497 Nicholas J. Wittner
Cause No.: 89-L-122 Circuit Court Madison County
Set for Trial: April 1990
Summary: Date of Accident: 10/21/1988. Near a slag pit at Granite City Steel Corporation in Granite City, IL. Deceased, Alan Little, a Granite City employee, was working near the slag pit when a Terex truck owned by St. Louis Slag and operated by its employee, Charles Wells, struck and ran over deceased.

HARTLEIN, DAVID v GENERAL MOTORS CORP., et al
Amount of Suit: Excess of $15,000.00
Attorney: Amiel Cueto
File No.: GM 115665 Silverman
Cause No.: 89-L-444 Circuit Court St. Clair County
Set for Trial: 2/22/1994
Summary: Date of Accident: 6/15/1987. Near Old Rt.40 in Madison County, IL. Plaintiff was working near truck when an outriger on the truck crushed his foot.

SJARDA, RICHARD H. v SHELL OIL COMPANY
Amount of Suit: $3,000,000.00
Attorney: Rex Carr
Cause No.:   89-L-273 Circuit Court Madison County
Set for Trial: 4/1/1991
Summary: Suit for malicious interference of contract and fraud.

JOY, KENNETH SR., et al v GENERAL MOTORS CORP., et al
Amount of Suit: $5,000,000.00
Attorney: P - Robert A Wulff; W. Joy - Charles F. Kirksey, Jr.
File No.:   GM 127821
Cause No.:   892-5584 Division 1, Circuit Court City of St. Louis
Summary: Date of Accident: 7/6/1988. Callaway County, MO on I-70. Willetta Joy was driving her 1985 Chevrolet when it collided with a vehicle drive by Roger Forsberg. Willetta's daughter, Maria Anita Joy, sustained a perforated colon allegedly the reuslt of the seatbelt. Maria died and her father, Kenneth Joy, Sr. brought suit against the healthcare providers and both drivers for wrongful death. Willetta Joy has filed a cross-claim against GM and the dealership, Don Brown Chevrolet Buick.

SQUIRES, PAMELA v J.C. PENNEY & MONTGOMERY ELEVATOR CCOMPANY (Commercial Union)
Amount of Suit: Excess of $15,000.00
Attorney: Frederick Steiger
File No.:   Wil Melendez
Cause No.:   85-L-688 Circuit Court Madison County
Set for Trial: 6/13/1988
Summary: Date of Accident: 3/9/1985. J.C. Penney store at Alton Square in Alton, IL. Plaintiff going "UP" exclator, fell as she stepped off the escalator.

AKEMAN, STEVEN, et al v UPJOHN
Amount of Suit: $100,000.00; Pnitive - $10,000,000.00
Attorney: Bruce Cook
Cause No.: 85-5538 USDC Souther District
Summary: Tetracycline Case.

BLAZINIC v UPJOHN, et al
Attorney: Husch, Eppenberger, et al
Cause No.: USDC 85-5628 Souther District
Summary: Tetracycline Case.

BLAZINIC, ROBERT, et al v UPJOHN, et al
Attorney: Cook
Cause No.: 85-3505 USDC E. St Louis
Summary: Tetracycline Case.

BAER, VICKIE, et al v UPJOHN
Amount of Suit: $100,000.00; Punitive - $10,000,000.00
Attorney: Bruce Cook
Cause No.: 85-5539 USDC Southern District
Summary: Tetracycline Case.

BARNES, DEBORAH v UPJOHN
Cause No.: 85-L-1007 Circuit Court St. Clair County
Summary: Tetracycline Case.

HELM, SUZANNE, et al v UPJOHN
Attorney: Bruce Cook
Cause No.: 85-3504 USDC E. St. Louis
Summary: Tetracycline Case.

MILLER, MARK v THE UPJOHN COMPANY, et al
Amount of Suit: $500,000.00
Attorney: Davidson, Schleuter & Mandel
Cause No.: 83-L-807 Circuit Court Madison County
Summary: Product Liability case involving tetracycline. Plaintiffs claim that their teeth were damaged as a result of using products containing tetracycline.

LUBBERS, DELBERT v P & D (See also Nottingham)
Amount of Suit: $40,000,000.00
Attorney: Robert D. Owen
File No.: 87-3219 USDC E. St. Louis
Summary: RICO case.

DEWITT, EARL E. v JOY MANUFACTURING COMPANY
Amount of Suit: Excess of $15,000.00
Attorney: Tom Keefe
File No.: 11-12-114 Dennis Morgenstern
Cause No.: 85-5484 USDC Alton, IL
Summary: Date of Accident: 3/11/1985. Zeigler Coal Co., Sparta, IL. Shuttle car caused low back injury

COSEY, RICHARD C., et al v METRO-EAST SANITARY DISTRICT v PFIZER PIGMENTS INC
Attorney: P - Kolker, Steegh, Younge, Cueto
Cause No.: 87-L-192; 86-L-1186;
86-L-1182 Circuit Court St. Clair County
Summary: Defense of negligence action.

HERZING, LARRY E. v NATIONAL AUTO SUPPLY CO., & EATON CORP., v CERRO COPPER PRODUCTS
Amount of Suit: Excess of $15,000.00
Attorney: P - John C. Webster;
                    National Auto - Dunham, Boman & Leskera;
                    Easton - John McMullin
File No.:   Western General 8701-0034-EL
Cause No.:   86-L-306 Circuit Court Madison County
Set for Trial: 9/12/1988
Summary: Date of Accident: 6/19/1984. Product Liability case involving a Synflex industrial hose which was being used on a bulblock. Hose manufactured by Eaton, distributed to Cerro Copper by National Auto. Plaintiff, an employee of Cerro, was operating a bulblock when the Synflex hose exploded resulting in injury to Plaintiff's right hand.

HARBAUGH, HAROLD & RUTH v VOLKSWAGEN OF AMERICA, INC.
Amount of Suit: Excess of $15,000.00
Attorney: Paul J. Passanante
File No.:   24C04724 (89) Bill Guida
Cause No.:   922-10306 Division 1, City of St. Louis
Summary: Date of Accident: 7/23/1992. Product Liability case involving 1989 VW Jetta GL. Plaintiff claims a defective restraint system. On Highway 40 near Phelps Road, Kansas City, MO. Plaintiff, traveling east on Rt. 40, involved in collision.

JOHNSON, CAROL A. v JOY MANUFACTURING CO.
Amount of Suit: Excess of $15,000.00
Attorney: Thomas Q. Keefe, Jr.
File No.:   11-12-088 Dennis Morgenstern
Cause No.:   88-4173 USDC
Summary: Date of Accident: 1/13/1983. Wabash Mine of Amax Coal Co. at Keensburg, Wabash County, IL. Product Liability case involving a "Joy Buggy." Plaintiff was operating buggy when it struck an obstruction throwing her about in the vehicle.

EAGLE ROCK DRYWALL CONTRACTORS v TEXAS-CAPITAL CONTRACTORS, INC.
Amount of Suit: $17,249.00
Attorney: Edward J. Blake, Jr. & Eric M. Rhein
Cause No.: 90-L-1224 Circuit Court St. Clair County
Summary: Contract action for work done at Scott Airforce Base.

PHILLIPS, SHEILA v GENERAL MOTORS CORPORATION, et al.
Amount of Suit: Excess $15,000.00
Attorney: Thomas Q. Keefe
File No.: 127313
Cause No.: 90-L-322 Circuit Court St. Clair County
Summary: Date of Accident: 3/5/1990. Product Liability case involving 1989 Oldsmobile Cutlass. 5:40 AM Plantiff, driving on Floraville Road in St. Clair County, IL, lost control of car. He alleges engine died, door came open, restraint system failed.

MYRACLE, DONALD v HYSTER COMPANY
Amount of Suit: $49,000.00
Attorney: Bernie Ysursa
File No.: 88-190
Cause No.: 90-L-1005 Circuit Court Madison County
Summary: Date of Accident: 12/8/1988. Product Liability case involving 1979 Hyster forklift Model S40C. Plaintiff injured when forklift rolled into him. Planitiff claims that forklift slipped into gear.

RUSSELL HURSEY v RYDER TRUCK RENTAL, INC., O'FALLON RENTAL, INC., GENERAL MOTORS CORPORATION and SERVICE, BRAKE AND CLUTCH, INC., a corporation
Amount of Suit: $15,000.00
Attorney: Bernie Ysursa
File No.: 90-L-557 St. Clair County
Summary: Date of Accident: Assigned to Bill Schmitt. Closed

McGINNIS, DOROTHY L. v FRANK BOMMARITO, INC. v GENERAL MOTORS CORPORATION
Amount of Suit: Property damage suit
Attorney: Sanford Goffstein, Clayton
File No.: 138119 Royal Kettwich
Cause No.: 21C88-07024 Circuit Court St. Louis
Summary: Property damage suit.

BROCHE, JANET K. v JOSEPH RAGLIN v GENERAL MOTORS CORP.
Attorney: P - Scott Dixon; Raglin - Richard Gibson
File No.: 128356; Royal 6350000137
Cause No.: IL-90-LM-187 Circuit Court Madison County
Summary: Date of Accident: 5/3/1988. Product Liability case involving 1987 Chevrolet Blazer. Accident occurred on the Clark bridge in Alton, IL. Plaintiff, driving her 1988 maroon Mercury Topaz in a northerly direction on the bridge when she was rear ended by Defendant Raglin who was driving a 1987 blue Chevrolet Blazer

TELLOR TONY v GENERAL MOTORS CORPORATION
Amount of Suit: Excess $15,000.00
Attorney: Donald Brandon; J.C. Micthell
File No.: 130483; Royal 163500002297
Cause No.: 90-L-111 Circuit Court Williamson County; 90-4166 USDC
Set for Trial: 2/3/1992
Summary: Date of Accident: 5/11/1990. Product Liability case involving 1978 Chevrolet C-10 pickup. I-57 near milepost 27 in Union County, IL. Plaintiff was driving the pickup south on I-57 when he swerved to avoid an animal and hit a concrete culvert. Plaintiff claims that the seat belt was defective.

WOLTERING, DAVID R. Admr. Of Estate of Stacey Lee Grace, Deceased v OUTBOARD MARINE CORPORATION
Amount of Suit:	Excess $15,000.00
Attorney:	Robert Gregory & Barbara Joiner
Cause No.:	90-L-193 Circuit Court Madison County
Summary:	Date of Accident: 4/27/1989. 4:00 PM on Mississippi River at or near mile marker 222 in St. Charles County, MO. Stacey Lee Grace was passenger in a boat operated by Timothy Heuer. She was thrown from the boat and struck by the propeller of the boat's Evinrude outboard motor. She died sometime later.

DOUGLAS, ELIZABETH v TOYOTA MOTOR SALES, et al
Amount of Suit:	Excess $15,000.00
Attorney:	Carr, Korein, et al (Richard Jones)
Cause No.:	90-L-1253 Circuit Court Belleville, IL
Summary:	Date of Accident: 11/28/1988. Product Liability case involving 1988 Toyotal Tercel. 2:12 PM Plaintiff, driving Toyota on US Rte. 50 east of IL Rte. 158 in St. Claire County when she was involved in a head on collision with another vehicle. Plaintiff claims that the Toyota was unreasonably dangerous and negligently designed in that the restraint system failed, and the vehicle was not equipped with an air bag.

HALL, RON v GENERAL MOTORS CORP. and RON WARD CHEVROLET COMPANY
Amount of Suit:	Excess $15,000.00
Attorney:	Brockton Lockwood
Cause No.:	90-L-117 Circuit Court Williamson City, Marion, IL
Set for Trial:	5/18/1993
Summary:	Date of Accident: 6/12/1989. 1988 Chevrolet Van. Plaintiff claims that on Monday, 6/12/89 he sustained injuries when the van burst into flames as he was driving it.

STANHAUS, DALE and KAREN v SCHMITT CHEVROLET and GENERAL MOTORS CORPORATION
Amount of Suit: Excess $15,000.00
Attorney: Carl Runge
Cause No.:   90-L-793 Circuit Court St. Clair County
Summary: Breach of Warranty case

JAMISON, KAREN Admr., etc. v GENERAL MOTORS CORPORATION. (See also Flanagan v. GM)
Amount of Suit: Excess $15,000.00
Attorney: P Wuller, Freeark, etc.
Cause No.:   90-L-288 Circuit Court St. Clair County
Set for Trial: 9/14/1992
Summary: Date of Accident: 8/14/1989. Plaintiff, driving a 1987 Gm Model 7000 tractor. Wrongful death case resulting from an accident on US Hwy. 51 near its intersectoin with IL Rt. 177 in Washington County, IL. Plaintiff's decedent operating a tractor-trailer truck in a northerly direction on US Rt. 51 when he collided with a tractor-trailer truck being operated by David D. Flanagan. Plaintiff claims that the brakes on the GM Model 7000 tractor were defective.

CAIRO, CITY OF v BUNGE CORPORATION
Amount of Suit: Excess $15,000.00
Attorney: P - James F. Flummer; P - Robert Keats
Cause No.:   90-4073 USDC Benton
Summary: Date of Accident: 3/16/1988. 6:50 AM at the pump house at Cairo, IL. There was an explosion at the old pump house. Plaintiff claims that hexane entered the sewer system from the Bunge plant causing the explosion.

BECKER, BARBARA, Special Admr. of the estate of DANNY BECKER, deceased, v THE UPJOHN COMPANY, et al
Amount of Suit: Excess $15,000.00
Attorney: Joseph Bartholomew
File No.:   90-I-390 Circuit Court St. Clair County
Cause No.:   12/9/1991
Set for Trial: 3/5/1983
Summary: Date of Accident: Plaintiff's decedent took a Medrol tablet which caused him to hallucinate and become disoriented and depressed so that he committed suicide.

TAYLOR, ALLEN C. v HUNT VALVE COMPANY, INC. and HYDRAULICS, INC.
Amount of Suit: Excess $15,000.00
Attorney: Morris B. Chapman & Assoc., Ltd.
Cause No.:   90-L-1522 Circuit Court Madison County
Summary: Product Liability case involving a "plunger." The plunger was designed and manufactured by the Hunt Valve Co. and rechromed by Hydraulics, Inc. The plunger was used in a piece of equipment at Granite City Steel Co. The Plaintiff is an employee of Granite City Steel Co. and was injured when the plunger failed.

HAWKEY, KATHY v. THE PRUDENTIAL INSURANCE COMPANY of AMERICA, MAY DEPARTMENT STORES COMPANY and MONTGOMERY ELEVATOR COMPANY
Amount of Suit: Less than $15,000.00
Attorney: Gregory Shevlin; Montgomery - Fred Forquer
File No.:   GB #36740-43436
Cause No.:   io-L-632 Circuit Court St. Clair County
Set for Trial: 1/25/1993
Summary: Date of Accident: 8/25/1988. Product Liability Case involving escalator at St. Clair Square. Plaintiff caught her hand in escalator.

BUTTS, RANDY, et al v JOY MANUFACTURING COMPANY
Amount of Suit: Excess $15,000.00
Attorney: Tom Keefe, Jr.
File No.:   11-12-81 Dennis Morgenstern
Cause No.:   91-L-1301 Circuit Court St. Clair County
Set for Trial: 6/7/1993
Summary: Date of Accident: 9/25/1981. Crown #2 mine of Freeman United Coal Mining Co., Virden, Macoupin County, IL. Product Liability case involving a "Joy Buggy." Plaintiff, operating a Joy Buggy when he ran over a rock row bouncing him around

THEODORE C. SCHMIDT and UELA SCHMIDT v MARY E. KRACK and NISSAN MOTOR CORPORATION IN USA
Amount of Suit: Excess $15,000.00
Attorney: Stephen Stephenson, Lakin Law Firm;
                    Co-D - Mike Constance
File No.:   Nissan NO. 08827
Cause No.:   2-L-0264 St. Clair County
Summary: Date of Accident: 5/12/1990. Product Liability case involving 1985 Nissan King Cab pickup. Plaintiff claims defective seat. 6:30 AM at intersection of N-W Little Oak Lane and E-W East B, Shiloh Township, St. Clair County. Plaintiff, southbound on Little Oak, struck by Co-Defendant east on East B.

McBRIDE v SPYTKOWSKI v MITSUBISHI
Amount of Suit: Excess $15,000.00
Attorney: P - Tom Rich; Co-D - Mike Reda
Cause No.:   92-891-WLB USDC, Southern District
Summary: Date of Accident: 10/5/1992. Product Liability case involving 1992 Mitsubishi Mirage. Intersection of Rt. 15 and 42nd Street, Alorton, IL. Plaintiff, traveling east on 15 in Mitsubishi Mirage and Co-Defendant, traveling west on Rt. 15, when Co-Defendant made left turn in front of Plaintiff. Co-Defendant filed a third party complaint against Mitsubishi alleging inadequate restraint and seat system.

RIX, STANLEY v KNOLL INTERNATIONAL
Amount of Suit: Excess $15,000.00
Attorney: Steve Ferguson
File No.:   96D 37912 Henry Schluter
Cause No.:   92-L-70 Circuit Court Williamson County, Marion, IL
Summary: Date of Accident: 4/3/1990. Product Liability case involving chair manufactured by Defendant. Peoples Bank of Marion, IL. Plaintiff sat in the chair when it fell over injuring Plaintiff.

TAMEZ, OSCAR v GENERAL MOTORS CORPORATION, et al
Amount of Suit: Excess $15,000.00
Attorney: Chas. J. Hughes
File No.:   66794 Doug Brown
Cause No.:   92-L-424 Circuit Court Madison County
Summary: Date of Accident: 7/14/1986. 2:45 PM intersection of IL State Rt. 121 and 98 near Morton, IL. Minor Plaintiff, a passenger in 1985 Cutlass Ciera drive by mother, Karen. Plaintiff claims GM negligent in manufacturing 1986 Oldsmobile Cutlass whose front passenger shoulder harness restraint was incapable of facilitating slack in the restraint.

LANTON, MICKEY v JOY, et al
Amount of Suit: Excess $15,000.00
Attorney: Tom Keefe, Jr.
File No.:   11-12-184 Larry Lepidi
Cause No.:   92-L-0037 St. Clair County, Belleveille
Set for Trial: 4/4/1991
Summary: Date of Accident: Product Liability case involving Joy shuttle car at Peabody Mine, St. Clair County. Plaintiff, a shuttle car operator, claims that the manual brake was defective causing his right foot to be crushed between shuttle car and rib.

CASH, CARL, et al v CHRYSLER CORPORATION, et al
Attorney: Judy Cates
File No.: 1004115 Lou Ann Van Der Wiele
Cause No.: 313-956-1449
Summary: Date of Accident: 5/27/1991. Product Liability case involving 1974 Jeep CJ-5. Death case - suit for survival and wrongful death. 11:30 AM on gravel road in Franklin County, IL. Deceased, a passenger in Jeep whose driver lost control causing it to hit a tree and roll over. Claim is for negligence based on oversteering, instability, crashworthiness, failed rollbar, inadequate warnings and instructions and improper advertisement re multiple-use.

ARNOLD, MICHELLE, et al v NISSAN MOTOR CORPORATION IN USA
Amount of Suit: Excess $15,000.00
Attorney: Bruce Cook
File No.: 10650-528 Bennett Traub
Cause No.: 9e-L-479 St. Clair County
Summary: Date of Accident: 12/18/1992. 8:45 PM Intersection Rt. 13 & 159, New Athens, IL. Product Liability case involving 1985 Nissan Sentra. Plaintiff's east on Rt 13 and Co-Defendant north on 156 collided. Six year old Michael Arnold in reclined passenger seat is paralyzed from waist down.

ROBERT BOLK v GROVE WORLD WIDE, UP-RIGHT AERIAL PLATFORMS and FORD MOTOR COMPANY
Amount of Suit: Excess $15,000.00
Attorney: Tom Keefe, Jr.
Cause No.: 93-576 USDC East St. Louis
Set for Trial: Nov-94
Summary: Date of Accident: 11/9/1989. Product Liability case involving hydraulic scaffold "Flying Tiger." Plaintiff, working on scaffold at Ford warehouse when he fell.

CARPENTER, CHERYL v ALTON GAMIN COMPANY v MONTGOMERY ELEVATOR
Amount of Suit: Excess $15,000.00
Attorney: P - Hugh Talbert; 3P - Gordon Broom
File No.:   GAB 617000-05008 Tim Duin
Cause No.:   93-L-751 Madison County
Summary: Date of Accident: 3/29/1992. Jones Act case. 10:15 AM Alton Belle. Plaintiff, a crew member in housekeeping, fell when elevator malfunctioned. Plaintiff filed a Jones Act case against Alton Belle which sues Montgomery for contribution.

DANDRIDGE, FRANCES v JOY MANUFACTURING COMPANY
Attorney: Robert Nelson
Cause No.:   92-L-628 Circuit Court St. Clair County
Set for Trial: 5/24/1989
Summary: Date of Accident: Plaintiff claims she was injured while employed by Peabody Coal Co. at the Baldwin Underground Mine in St. Clair County. Plaintiff claims she was operating the shuttle car in Unit 5 when she hit a pothole causing her to be injured.

SABRELINER CORPORATION v JOY TECHNOLOGIES INC.
Amount of Suit: $100,714.56
Attorney: Reed Sugg, Shephard, Sandberg
File No.:   1-12-059
Cause No.:   591129 Circuit Court St. Louis County
Summary: Suit to collect for repairs made by Plaintiff on Joy's corporate Sabreliner airplane.

JOHNSTON, LEE ANN v DIAMOND-STAR MOTORS CORP. et al
Amount of Suit: Excess $15,000.00
Attorney: B. Jay Dowling
Cause No.: 91-L-746 Circuit Court St. Clair County
Set for Trial: 11/14/1994
Summary: Date of Accident: 6/16/1990. Product Liability case involving a 1990 Plymouth Laser automobile. 2 AM Plaintiff, a passenger in automobile driven by Defendant, Thomas Sumner. Sumner was driving in a southerly direction on the Floraville Road near lower Saxtown Road in St. Clair County. The vehicle left the roadway and Plaintiff was ejected. Plaintiff claims that the passive restraint system was defective.

YOUNG, MICHELLE, etc. v MONTGOMERY ELEVATOR COMPANY
Amount of Suit: Excess $15,000.00
Attorney: Ted Barylske - Wisemand, Shikewitz, et al
File No.: GAB 36740-44473 Tim Duin
Cause No.: 93-L-1205 Madison County
Summary: Date of Accident: 3/5/1989. Alton Square, Alton, IL. 12 year old Plaintiff riding "UP" escalator manufactured by Westinghouse caught shoestring. Montgomery Elevator had service contract for escalator.

HOFFMAN, DWAYNE FRED v JOY TECHNOLOGIES INC and ROGER HINES
Amount of Suit: Excess $15,000.00
Attorney: Tom Keefe, Jr.
File No.: 11-12-180
Cause No.: 93-L-360
Summary: Date of Accident: 3/31/1989. Product Liability case involving a Joy shuttle car. Peabody Coal Co. underground mine. Plaintiff claims that while he was operating shuttle car it hit a hole or other obstruction causing him to be bounced from the shuttle car.

HOLT, TIMOTHY V. v JOY MANUFACTURING COMPANY
Amount of Suit: Excess $15,000.00
Attorney: Lloyd Cueto
File No.:   11-12-189 Larry Lepidi
Cause No.:   i3-L0113 Belle
Set for Trial: April 1994
Summary: Date of Accident: 3/7/1992. Monterey Coal Company #2 mine, Albers, IL. Plaintiff, operating a shuttle car when it hit a hole causing him to be bounced from the seat.

CLEMENTS, PRISCILLA v JOYCE GRAY and GENERAL MOTORS CORPORATION
Amount of Suit: Excess $15,000.00
Attorney: Bernard Ysursa
Cause No.:   93-L-1053 Madison County
Summary: Date of Accident: 1/7/1993. Product Liability case involving 1991 Chevrolet Camaro. I-270 at intersection with 367 in St. Louis County, MO. Plaintiff, driving Camero west on I-270 when collided with Co-Defendant vehicle. Plaintiff claims the airbag failed to disperse enhancing her injuries.

Conclusion

As previously noted, the cases referred to in this booklet represent only 416 of the 1,248 cases referred to me after November, 1958, when I joined Pope and Driemeyer and none of the approximate 200 cases referred to me prior to joining Pope and Driemeyer.

Preparation is the key and most important factor in handling any lawsuit. In defending a product liability case, the trial lawyer's client is the product, i.e., the plaintiff lawyer's target. In order to defend the target product the trial lawyer must learn every detail about the manufacture, purpose, reasonable expectation, etc., of the product along with scientific laws supporting defensive conclusions. I defended automobiles of all kinds which included steering gears, tires, air bags, metal fatigue, stability, crashworthiness, accident reconstruction, energy absorbing steering columns, overall design, potential fuel-fed fire protection, fuel tanks, seat belts and other restraints, etc. I defended helicopters, pharmaceutical drugs, batteries, underground mine equipment, hair dye, tampons, trucks of all kinds, farm tractors, escalators, etc., etc.

In order to defend such cases it was necessary to consult with and be educated by topflight experts. During my career, I worked with experts from all over the U.S.A., as well as England, Germany and Japan. This was very important for preparation in presenting their testimony at trial, as well as enabling me to examine adverse experts at trial or deposition. On one occasion, I conducted my own experiment by riding out with the coal on a conveyor belt from deep underground of a Peabody Coal mine. I was told to keep my head low and I did.

Preparation is the key to handling any lawsuit successfully.

Tom Coghill

www.ingramcontent.com/pod-product-compliance
Lightning Source LLC
Chambersburg PA
CBHW080657190526
45169CB00006B/2153